This wonderful book gives us a picture of the vital part women have played in redemptive history. It is a great resource to help Christ followers see how God has used women and the prominent and strategic role they have played throughout history.

TOMMY LEE, president, Resource Global

This book is a wonderful gift to a... y from Scripture how
incredib   derstanding the full
biblical s   d make today.

f *How (Not) To Read the*
ent, Western Seminary

This is th   .n recommending to
everyone. Get ready for nonstop aha moments.

CHRISTINE CAINE, founder, Propel Women and A21

A transformative journey into God's saving story! God chose to use women—many of whom were mistreated or ignored—at key junctures in redemptive history. These marginalized women prove to be anything but marginal within God's purposes. They act boldly and speak wisely at pivotal points in God's story, teaching us who God is and who we must become.

MATTHEW W. BATES, author of *Why the Gospel?*; professor of New Testament, Northern Seminary

Why do the biblical authors put women in such prominent and powerful positions in the world of the ancient Near East? Ingrid Faro steps back to show us the arc of female operatives and their central role in God's plan for salvation. Her lucid insights drawn from decades of her scholarship point out the pattern of female dauntlessness across the pages of Scripture. We have been waiting for an authoritative, holistic, and easy-to-read book that does justice to the prominence of women at the renowned junctures of biblical history. This is that book, and it is a joyous read.

DRU JOHNSON, Wycliffe Hall, University of Oxford

Many of us grew up thinking that the Bible focuses on men of faith—like Abraham, Moses, David, and the male disciples. We knew there are women in Bible stories, but we were taught to ignore them. Faro and Dalrymple demonstrate that, time and again, women are not only there at key pivotal moments in the story of redemption but also play major roles, by God's calling and grace. It's long past time these stories were told and cherished, for the blessing and encouragement of everyone in the church.

NIJAY K. GUPTA, Julius R. Mantey Professor of New Testament, Northern Seminary; author of *Tell Her Story*

In *Redeeming Eden,* Ingrid Faro serves a hearty meal to readers hungry for biblical food by combining her knowledge of women in the Bible, her solid grasp of narrative, and her Hebrew textual acumen. She creates the perfect feast, inviting readers to savor some familiar stories—and discover a few they might have missed—as they encounter anew the God who created, calls, and commissions women.

SANDRA L. GLAHN, professor of media arts and worship, Dallas Theological Seminary

I wish I'd had this book as a young woman. I hope tens of thousands of Christians will read it and discover the strategic role that women play in God's redemptive story. Dr. Faro's careful reading of the Hebrew text yields many fresh insights and unravels many harmful stereotypes about Bible women. I couldn't put it down!

DR. CARMEN JOY IMES, associate professor of Old Testament, Biola University; author of *Becoming God's Family: Why the Church Still Matters*

For too long, women in Scripture have been interpreted as one dimensional and passive. Dr. Ingrid Faro's deep scholarship and contextual explanations reveal that women were dynamic participants in God's work of salvation. I was particularly encouraged by the way she incorporated Hebrew in accessible ways for lay people.

LARK KELSEY, PhD student, at Baylor University's George W. Truett Theological Seminary

Redeeming Eden invites readers into a sweeping and sacred journey through the Old Testament—one that highlights the often-overlooked stories of faithful, courageous women who helped shape God's redemptive plan. With both depth and accessibility, Ingrid and Joyce trace the legacy of godly female leaders and offer fresh insight into their significance within the larger biblical narrative. This beautifully researched resource is more than a study—it's a celebration of the women whose obedience and strength played a vital role in God's unfolding story. *Redeeming Eden* is a heartfelt companion for anyone longing to see Scripture through a fuller, richer lens.

KAT ARMSTRONG, Bible teacher, podcast host of *Holy Curiosity*,
and author of the Storyline Bible Study Series

Redeeming Eden is a theologically rich and compelling work that reintroduces us to the fierce, faith-filled women whose witness is intricately woven into the fabric of redemptive history. With prophetic clarity, Ingrid and Joyce invite the church to recognize what God has always seen—the enduring power of his daughters walking in courage, justice, and a strength that is both humble and heroic.

NOEMI CHAVEZ, pastor, Revive Church

So often the incredible women in biblical history have been interpreted as villains, vixens, or divas. At long last, Ingrid Faro and Joyce Koo Dalrymple have brought us a faithful, thoughtful, and robust interpretation of women in Scripture, showing how God's faithfulness in and through them has served the *missio Dei*, with power.

AUBREY SAMPSON, pastor, church planter, podcaster,
and author of *What We Find in the Dark*

Redeeming Eden is an example of a rare book that is replete with rigorous scholarship but presented in a way that is understandable and meaningful. Readers will learn a great deal, be corrected in some false assumptions, and then be able to apply what they learn through the insightful guides for discussion and prayer. I cannot wait to return to this book as a rich personal resource and recommend it to many who need to know the powerful way God delighted to work with women throughout Israel's history.

AMY PEELER, Kenneth T. Wessner Chair in
Biblical Studies, Wheaton College

How Women
in the Bible
Advance the Story
of Salvation

REDEEMING
EDEN

Ingrid Faro

with Joyce Koo Dalrymple

ZONDERVAN
REFLECTIVE

ZONDERVAN REFLECTIVE

Redeeming Eden
Copyright © 2025 by Ingrid Faro

Published by Zondervan, 3950 Sparks Drive SE, Suite 101, Grand Rapids, Michigan, 49546, USA. Zondervan is a registered trademark of The Zondervan Corporation, L.L.C., a wholly owned subsidiary of HarperCollins Christian Publishing, Inc.

Requests for information should be addressed to customercare@harpercollins.com.

Zondervan titles may be purchased in bulk for educational, business, fundraising, or sales promotional use. For information, please email SpecialMarkets@Zondervan.com.

ISBN 978-0-310-16932-1 (audio)

Library of Congress Cataloging-in-Publication Data

Names: Faro, Ingrid author | Dalrymple, Joyce Koo, 1976– author
Title: Redeeming Eden : how women in the Bible advance the story of salvation / Ingrid Faro with Joyce Koo Dalrymple.
Description: Grand Rapids, Michigan : Zondervan, [2025] | Includes index.
Identifiers: LCCN 2025011773 (print) | LCCN 2025011774 (ebook) | ISBN 9780310169307 paperback | ISBN 9780310169314 ebook
Subjects: LCSH: Women in the Bible | Women—Biblical teaching | Bible. Old Testament—Criticism, interpretation, etc. | Christian women—Religious life
Classification: LCC BS575 .F257 2025 (print) | LCC BS575 (ebook) | DDC 220.9/2082—dc23/eng/20250530
LC record available at https://lccn.loc.gov/2025011773
LC ebook record available at https://lccn.loc.gov/2025011774

Cover design: Darren Welch Design
Cover art: © 2Windspa / Getty Images
Interior design: Denise Froehlich

Printed in the United States of America

25 26 27 28 29 LBC 5 4 3 2 1

Contents

Foreword

The Bible is intended to be read in community. That doesn't just mean reading it when gathered with others, although that is a very good thing to do. To read the Bible in community means honoring Scripture as a gift God gave *through* his Spirit-filled people, *for* his Spirit-filled people. Some of us live with the illusion that our faith can be sustained with private devotion, and pop Christianity often celebrates the false trinity of Me, God, and the Bible. But even when reading the Bible alone, we are relying on the invisible community of scholars and translators behind the text, as well as the saints who wrote, preserved, and transmitted it across the ages and oceans. By God's design, a community placed the Bible in our hands, and when we open it, we also need the help of a community to read and apply it.

When we reject this truth and read the Bible in isolation, we are often unaware of the assumptions and blind spots we carry that cause us to misinterpret the text. Nowhere is that more apparent than when reading the stories of women in Scripture. Most Bible readers will acknowledge that modern American culture is very different from the ancient Near East, but how these differences apply to the roles of women is often ambiguous at best. In other words, when modern readers encounter female characters in the Bible, many of us simply don't know what we don't know. Therefore, we may unconsciously import modern assumptions about gender into biblical stories, resulting in a skewed vision of female characters, or we may miss the story's original intent altogether.

Thankfully, we can correct these errors and illuminate the text of Scripture more brightly by welcoming Ingrid Faro and Joyce Koo Dalrymple into our Bible reading community. Their scholarship and accessible teaching help us see the women of the Bible as they were intended and gently prompt us to recognize the cultural biases we have carried into these stories for too long. It is not an exaggeration to say that the insights in this book will change the way you understand not only specific stories but also the larger arc of the biblical narrative and the character of the God directing it.

Perhaps what I appreciate most about *Redeeming Eden* is the way it respects the broader literary context of the Bible, even while examining the essential details of specific stories and women. It may seem contradictory, but *Redeeming Eden* respects the role of women in Scripture by not putting them at the center of Scripture's story. Neither does it place men at the center (which is a far more common error). Instead, it recognizes that God himself is the main character of this narrative and that he employs both women and men to achieve his purposes and unveil his character.

Many Americans miss this seemingly obvious fact because they have been taught to approach the Bible as a manual of instruction. They view it as a divine depository of practical wisdom for life. We see this popular approach elevated by three-point alliterated sermons and youth ministry clichés such as "B.I.B.L.E. stands for Basic Instructions Before Leaving Earth."

If we believe the Bible is a manual, we will naturally approach the stories of women in Scripture with the practical questions our culture is asking about women: What roles should women have in the community of God's people? What does godly femininity look like? How should women and men relate in a community and a marriage? How do women navigate responsibilities inside and outside the household? How do women use, abuse, and respond to power? Questions like these are often debated today, and the Bible-as-manual approach attempts to settle them by citing specific chapters and verses. Thankfully, Faro and Dalrymple avoid this over-traveled path.

The fact that this approach to Scripture has not ended the arguments about women in the twenty-first century reveals at least three things. First, the Bible may not speak with one, uniform voice about women. Opinions on both sides of every debated issue regarding women can draw from different stories, characters, and passages to support their positions. Second, the Bible's original authors may not have been asking the same questions about women that our culture is asking. As an Old Testament scholar once told me in a moment of interpretive frustration, "Maybe you should stop asking questions the text doesn't want to answer." Third, the popular American approach of reading the Bible as a self-help resource may have significant shortcomings. Perhaps this ancient book wasn't given to us primarily as a user manual for human beings.

Rather than just a manual, I believe the Bible is primarily a window. Yes, there is practical instruction to be drawn from Scripture and applied, but there is also much more to it. *Through it*, we see who God is, what he is like, and how his people have interacted with him through the ages. As this vision becomes clearer and transforms our imaginations, it produces a wisdom in us beyond mere lists of axioms and life principles. And if we believe the primary goal of the Bible is God's self-revelation to his people, then we will ask very different questions of its female characters. Rather than "What does this story teach me about *femininity?*" we will ask, "What does this story teach me about *divinity?*" In other words, we will approach the women of the Bible to learn about God, not about gender.

By taking this approach, Faro and Dalrymple not only honor the Bible but also dignify the women within it as equal and indispensable instruments of God's self-revelation. By keeping God himself at the center of Scripture, rather than our self-interest or cultural debates, we also resist the temptation to exalt Adam over Eve, Abraham over Sarah, or David over Bathsheba. The male characters are not more important than the female, any more than one facet of a stained glass window is more critical than another. Only together, in their carefully placed contrasting colors and shapes, do we see the manifold glory of God. I hope the pages ahead will open your eyes to this beauty as they have mine.

SKYE JETHANI, author and cofounder of Holy Post Media

Acknowledgments

Thank you to Katya Covrett at Zondervan for passing my manuscript on to Dale Williams. And thank you to Dale for his encouragement, edits, and seeing the vision for *Redeeming Eden*, along with Kim Tanner for her important edits, Emily Bruff for marketing, and Liz England for her video work. The whole team has been supportive and fun to work with.

Huge thanks to Joyce Koo Dalrymple for joining me in this journey! Her wise edits and insightful comments throughout the writing of this book and her beautiful "Reflect on the Chapter," "Reflect on Your Life," "Take Your Bold Step," and "Breath Prayer" sections for each chapter contributed immensely to the quality of this book and the joy of writing it. To riff a bit on Psalm 133, how good and how pleasant it is when God's people work together in unity!

Thank you to all my students in Women in the Old Testament and especially Veronica Reeves, who became my TA and gave input and feedback on ideas and edits as I worked on my manuscript.

Thanks and glory be to God.

Introduction

Bold Women in God's Big Picture

R arely is a woman the main topic of a sermon or teaching outside of women's Bible study groups. This oversight has caused a dearth of insight into how important women are to God and his mission. This book traces a thread through Scripture that forms a cohesive narrative demonstrating that women initiate and advance key movements in redemptive history. These contributions go largely unnoticed in scholarship, teaching, and preaching. God values women. Therefore, God strategically works through overlooked and underestimated women and girls who responded bravely in difficult circumstances to change the history of the world.

Most of us have overlooked the role of women in advancing the storyline of the Bible and history. Hebrew Bible scholar Jacob Wright observes that in the historical and theological account of the Israelite people recorded in Scripture, "women introduce the major epochs and their central themes. . . . Indeed, women figure prominently across the entire biblical corpus: from the matriarchs who create the nation to Esther who saves it."[1] I too missed Scripture's significant portrayal of women until I began teaching a graduate class on women in the Old Testament. The first year I taught this class, it was the toughest course in my fifteen years of teaching because I didn't realize how many triggers it would set off among both the women and the men in the class. Since then, it's become my favorite class. I've learned to prepare for the traumas and triggers and to incorporate discussions about the misinformation and, frankly, wretched ways biblical women are often spoken about or ignored in the church. It was during this time, as I studied and prepared for my classes, that I began to see the pivotal placement of women in the Bible's storyline.

Each chapter in this book builds on the others, pointing toward a comprehensive theme that recognizes God's attention to women who were not looking for success or title. Often these biblical women were considered despised, foreigners, or of questionable value within Israelite society. These women weren't trying to be heroes. They simply took action to do what was right or just. Their unpretentious tenacity transformed history.

Most of these would be considered ordinary women. Some of the women may be unfamiliar to you. A few had positions of significance in their time. Though these women are rarely the main topic of conversations or preaching, they are honored in the pages of Scripture. Some of their reputations have been wrongfully sullied or vilified. We will acknowledge these women and, when needed, set their stories right.

I have no agenda to push and no axe to grind. My goal is to recount women whom God has deemed noteworthy through their strategic placement in the Bible, using clean exegesis, incorporating ancient Near Eastern cultural evidence and archaeological material, and reading within the canonical context. All of this background contributes to our understanding and interpretation. As such, this book is intended to be accessible to those with a general interest in women of the Bible and to those studying the subject academically, historically, or curiously.

Since beginning my biblical and theological studies in 2000, I've approached the role of women in Scripture prayerfully and curiously. Thirteen years of theological graduate study, including biblical Hebrew, Koine Greek, cognate (related) languages of Ugaritic, Aramaic, and Northwest Semitic inscriptions, have been complemented with learning from scholars who work extensively in Akkadian, Sumerian, Egyptian (hieroglyphics and hieratic), and archaeology. Having taught the Hebrew Bible/Old Testament now for sixteen years at five institutions, including biblical Hebrew through advanced exegesis for eleven years, and working alongside amazing colleagues, I have expanded the tools available in my research. All of this is undergirded with prayer and the commitment to be "approved to God" as one "accurately handling the word of truth" (2 Tim 2:15 NASB).

My tools for this exploration, therefore, are biblical Hebrew (the primary original language of the Old Testament), occasionally the Septuagint (the Greek translation of the Hebrew Bible around 200 BC), the Greek of the New Testament, archaeological and material culture, ancient law codes, and other scholarly research that sheds light on our understanding of the history and interpretation of the passages. We will dig into what the words and stories may have meant to the first hearers and readers of the biblical texts. We'll also trace the connections and recurring themes to uncover the roles and significance of these women within the broader biblical narrative.

Along the way, you'll discover the importance of women from God's perspective. Hopefully, you'll find refreshing insights that inspire men and women alike to be people of valor in the face of wrongs and bold in the presence of powers that would silence those who stand up for the dignity of others and themselves. In his work on the plot structure of Genesis, Todd Patterson observes, "Female characters in Genesis often take initiative that determines the next development in the narrative (e.g. Eve, Sarah, Tamar). This important theme has not received adequate attention even from feminist scholars and yet the plot-structure

provides fertile ground for new explorations."[2] This theme
(women initiating narrative movements) continues throughout
the plot structure of the Pentateuch and the Historical Books of
the Old Testament (the Torah and Former Prophets in the Hebrew
Bible).

Our exploration begins in Genesis 1 through 4, examining
the Hebrew words and structure of the biblical text to better
understand who woman is as an image bearer of God with man.
We investigate who women are designed to be from creation as
coregents with God and as partners with men in carrying out
God's mission from Eden to the rest of the earth.[3] We also look
at what happened to the liaison between woman and man in
the movement from Genesis 2 to 3. From Genesis 3 to the end of
Revelation, God is at work redeeming what was lost in Eden, and
the Bible shows us that women have a strategic role in advancing salvation history. Thus, throughout Scripture, women play an
ongoing and pivotal part in redeeming Eden.

From this foundational discussion, we progress and identify
the stories of some key individual women who initiate important
narrative movements in Scripture. There are many, many more
who aren't covered in this book. The following paragraphs sum-
marize the stories of a few of the women we will explore.

In Genesis 12 through 21, both Abraham and Sarah at times
act in faith and at times act in doubt. Ultimately, both need to
respond in faith when God promises them an heir, as Abraham is
one hundred years old and Sarah's womb is "dead" (Gen 18:11–14;
Rom 4:19; Heb 11:11–12). Their faith provides an early understanding of life coming from death.

Exodus begins with the sons of Jacob and the "fruitfulness"
of the Israelite women who are slaves in Egypt. The narrative
quickly turns its attention to two midwives who defy the orders
of the mightiest leader of the ancient Near East, the pharaoh.
They refuse to kill the baby slave boys. Then the story turns to

a mother, daughter, and princess who also defy the pharaoh's orders and work together to save one particular slave baby boy, who is initially nameless. After all, he's just the baby of slaves, of no consequence to the world. Although the pharaoh is afraid of the Israelite men revolting against him, he misses that the actions of brave women initiate his demise. Five women of different ages and backgrounds save the slave baby boy, who would be named Moses and become God's appointed deliverer of the slaves who form the nation of Israel.

In Exodus and Numbers, Miriam is recognized, along with Moses and Aaron, as one of the leaders who followed God and brought Israel out of Egypt. Miriam, like her brothers, had a significant moment of failure: Aaron in Exodus 32:1–35; Miriam in Numbers 12:1–15; and Moses in Numbers 20:8–13. Yet, also along with her brothers, she is honored for her role and acknowledged as a prophet: Aaron in Exodus 7:1; Miriam in Exodus 15:20; and Moses in Deuteronomy 18:18. The leadership of all three is spoken of in Micah 6:4.

The book of Joshua opens with the admonition to be strong and courageous and to be careful to do all that the Lord commands. Joshua 2 hints at questionable behavior of the two spies sent ahead of the troops into Jericho. But thanks to the bold, faith-filled words and actions of Rahab, a Canaanite woman of questionable occupation, the spies are delivered and Jericho is defeated. Rahab and her family become integrated into the people of Israel, with her becoming the wife of the Israelite Salmon and mother of Boaz, in the line of David and the Messiah (Ruth 4:21–22; Matt 1:5).

The book of Judges starts with the death of Joshua (Judg 2:6–10). After his death, Israel does evil in the sight of the Lord and serves the gods of Canaan. When the Israelites call out to the Lord, he sends judges to deliver them from their attackers and oppressors. In the Old Testament, only three figures are identified as both a judge and a prophet: Moses (Exod 18:13–27; Deut 18:18); Deborah (Judg 4:4); and Samuel, the last judge of Israel (1 Sam 7:6, 15–17; 3:20). Deborah, in cooperation with general Barak, delivers the Israelites from Jabin, king of Canaan, and his general Sisera, bringing Israel forty years of peace.

During the time of the judges, we also have the story of Ruth. She is routinely called a Moabite in the book bearing her name. Her bold confession and actions of faith in following Naomi, her Israelite mother-in-law, and the God of Israel bring her into the line of David and the Messiah (Ruth 4:16–22; Matt 1:5).

First Samuel opens with the story of Hannah, one of two wives of Elkanah, also during the time of the judges. The main priest at this time, Eli, sees her lips moving but making no sound, so he assumes Hannah is drunk as she silently implores the Lord for a child. Hannah's prayer is answered. Her firstborn, Samuel, restores national worship. He is the last judge and prophet in the Old Testament, initiating the monarchy by anointing first Saul and then David as king. Much later, the prayer of Mary, mother of Jesus, significantly mirror's Hannah's prayer.

First Kings continues the thread of redemptive history. While David is in his final days, he has ignored the kingdom's succession. The prophet Nathan and Bathsheba, mother of Solomon, step in. We finally hear Bathsheba's voice as she advocates for the fulfillment of God's promises regarding Solomon's kingship. Nathan's council and Bathsheba's courage secure the continuation of the messianic line through Solomon.

In the following chapters, we will delve into the details of the lives and times of these women. Some of them are famous; most are not. All of them inspire us to live better, be bolder, and trust God more deeply. They encourage us to work in cooperation with other women and men to save lives, deliver the oppressed, provide for the needy, and expand goodness in our world, whether or not anyone is watching.

The end of each chapter has questions to prompt you to reflect on the content, consider how the chapter applies to your life, and take potential action steps. These questions are intended to help you process what you've read individually or with others and prayerfully consider how God might want you to respond. Finally, each chapter concludes with a breath prayer to help you slow down and connect with God. This practice involves slowly breathing in and out while repeating a simple prayer several times following the rhythm of your breath.

Reflect on the Chapter

* What is the role of women in the storyline of the Bible and in redemptive history? Is this surprising to you? Why or why not?
* From this chapter, name a few specific ways women initiate and advance God's redemptive plan.

Reflect on Your Life

* God placed women in key junctures of redemptive history, which reveals how much God values women. In what ways have women been valued at your church, work, or community? In what ways have you seen women being undervalued?
* Who have been some women in your life who have inspired you to live better, be bolder, and trust God more deeply?
* What do you hope to learn or take away from this book?

Take Your Bold Step

* Write a thank you note to a woman who has inspired you.

- Share one thing you learned about how God values women with someone in your life.
- If you are a ministry leader, plan a lesson, Bible study, or sermon about one of the bold women in Scripture.

Breath Prayer

(Inhale)	Lord, open my eyes to see
(Exhale)	how you delight in women.

CHAPTER 1

Man and Woman as God's Image

GENESIS 1

The way a story begins is important. The beginning is how the author sets the scene and lays the foundation for how we read the rest of the book. Genesis 1 opens with "In the beginning God created the heavens and the earth." In the beginning, God had a plan. He wanted to manifest the spiritual realm within a physical universe and to express his being in the earth through us as his image bearers. We humans probably best understand this as imagining an idea, a concept, or an invention and, through a creative process, bringing our inner image into tangible reality.

Recently, I rewatched the movie *Hidden Figures*, about the first black women at NASA and their pivotal roles in sending the first man into space. The human ability to create what is not yet is expressed by Katherine Goble Johnson, as she says, "In my mind I'm already there."[1] An embellishment of Michelangelo's words about his creative process convey a similar idea: "I saw the angel in the marble and carved until I set it free."* Certainly some

---

* The source of these words is unknown, but perhaps a creative expansion from Michelangelo's letter to Benedetto Varchi, "*Io intendo scultura quella che si fa per forza di levare: quella che si fa per via di porre è simile alla pittura*" which is roughly translated, "I mean sculpture, that which is done by force of taking away: that which

human inventions and works of art happen by chance. More commonly, however, the creative process involves envisioning something that inspires actions to create something new. These creations are often an expression of our being or our character. With this in mind, we turn to the biblical story.

The Bible is a beautiful literary piece of art. It is also the most read book in the world. I believe it is divinely inspired to tell us about God, the world, and ourselves. If you question or don't accept the Bible as authoritative or inspired, then I invite you to join this exploration as a narrative project. The opening two chapters of the Bible describe God's creative process and give insight into his thoughts and character. As Catherine McDowell points out, "No biblical text has received more attention than the opening chapters of Genesis. In particular, the creation of humans in the image (*ṣelem*) and likeness (*dĕmût*) of God, as it is described in Genesis 1:26–27."[2] Indeed, how we read this passage is the foundation on which we must build our understanding of the rest of Scripture.

The stories we believe about who we are and where we come from shape our worldview and the way we see ourselves and value others. In Genesis 1 the character and inner life of God are expressed through his words and actions. Let's note these and compare them with other ancient Near Eastern stories of the making of the cosmos (cosmogeny) and the making of humans (anthropogeny).

God Creates in Community for Community

In reading through Genesis 1, we find layers of interconnected relationships, with no mention of any forces in conflict or in competition with the one God. God's work of creation was done in

---

is made by means of placing is similar to painting." See https://it.wikisource.org/wiki /Lettera_a_messer_Benedetto_Varchi.

community and for the sake of creating more community. The divine, the spiritual, the human, and the earthly communities are all designed to function together in harmony.

This one God, however, is multifaceted. The Creator acts through the community within himself, moving through his Spirit and speaking through his Word. God then reveals himself and his character through what he makes and in the way he makes them.

Although the Hebrew word for God, *Elohim*, is a plural noun, the verb "created" in Genesis 1:1 is singular. God is one and yet a complex, manifold God. Chief rabbi Jonathan Sacks says, "Elohim in the plural means, 'the One who is the totality of powers, forces and causes in the universe.' It refers to God as we experience Him in creation and its natural laws, as well as in justice and its moral laws."[3] A Hebrew word used elsewhere in the Bible for the universe, *olam*, "is connected to the verb meaning 'to hide' (see Lev 4:13; Deut 22:1). The physical world is a place in which the presence of God is real, yet hidden."[4]

This complex God is further described in the creation narrative as having a Spirit. The Spirit (or breath or wind) of God moved across the expansive deep (Gen 1:2). In Hebrew, the word "Spirit" (*ruakh*) is a singular, feminine noun. The actions of the Spirit, or breath force of God, in Genesis 1:2 can also be translated as the Spirit of God "fluttering" over the face of the waters "like a bird, that moves its wings back and forth."[5] The verb "to flutter" occurs also in Deuteronomy 32:11, describing an eagle that hovers, or flutters, over the baby birds in its nest. The God who conceives the idea of heavens and earth and imbues movement and breath through his Spirit also speaks, and his thoughts become reality. This complex God cooperates and communes in perfect unison between the power of his thoughts, movement of his Spirit, and force of his words. Birthing language pertaining to the creation of the world is echoed in Job 38:8–9 (NRSVue), when God asks Job,

"Who shut in the sea with doors
  when it burst out from the womb,
when I made the clouds its garment
  and thick darkness its swaddling band?"

The God of creation has community within himself.

We're not told how God created the heavenly realms before the universe was set in motion, but the Bible speaks of spiritual beings present at the birth of creation in Job 38:7 (NRSVue). God tells Job that when he created the universe, "the morning stars sang together and all the heavenly beings [lit. 'sons of Elohim'] shouted for joy." The Hebrew terms for "morning stars" and "sons of Elohim" are common expressions for nonhuman, spiritual beings who were created before the physical, earthly realm.[6] Our multifaceted God, Elohim, created the world in conversation with spiritual beings that he had created in his likeness. This is expressed in Genesis 1:26 (NRSVue): "Then God said, 'Let us make humans in our image, according to our likeness . . .'" W. Randall Garr demonstrates convincingly in his extensive work on this passage that when God "reveals his intention to make the human race," he is situated "in his divine community" of heavenly beings who are fully in unity and in "support of their leader."[7]

The process of creation unfolds over several days, each having a marked time. The seventh day, however, is unique. After God completes his creation and appoints humanity to represent him in the physical world, God ceases from his work of creation.[8] The interconnected layers of community are complete. The number six "represents the material, physical, secular."[9] The number seven has special significance in Hebrew understanding, indicating holiness, fullness, or perfection. The "seven-day" framework serves a double purpose. First, it speaks to the common ancient Near Eastern practice of using a "seven-day" framework as a literary devise for marking sacred time when describing building a temple for their god(s). The creation story in Genesis 1 is a "temple-inauguration" text. In other words, the universe is God's cosmic sanctuary, and the earth represents the physical place of his dwelling.[10] Second, the seven days of Genesis 1 provide a template for human society's work week.[11] Seven is also the number of times that God assesses his work: "God saw that it was good." With the seventh time, after creating humanity, he emphasizes that "it was very good."

The creation narrative can be described as "exalted prose."[12] Let's look in more detail at the final act, which many describe as the crown of creation: the making of humanity in Genesis 1:26–28.[13]

> Then God said, Let us make humanity as our image,[14] according to our likeness, so that they may have dominion in the realm of the fish of the sea, the birds in the sky, all the animals, and all the earth, and every moving thing that moves upon the earth.
>
> And God created humankind as his image, as the image of God he created it (humanity);[15] male and female he created them (humanity).[16]
>
> Then God blessed them, and God said to them, Be fruitful, and multiply, and fill the earth, and subdue it, and have dominion in the realm of the fish of the sea, and the birds in the sky, and every animal that moves upon the earth. (my translation)

The culmination of God's act of creating humanity proceeded in community, for community. As Carmen Joy Imes puts it, God made humanity in "teamwork," in consultation with "us": the "morning stars" and "sons of Elohim" in God's divine council.[17] The Hebrew word *ādām* (hereafter, just written as *adam*) in Genesis 1 and in most of the Hebrew Bible means humanity, not gendered "man." This is clear from verse 27, where God's creation of humanity (*adam*) is first identified with a singular pronoun and in the next clause within the same sentence is identified as "male and female" with a plural pronoun. Verse 28 continues with the double plural pronoun: "God blessed *them*, and God said to *them* . . ." (emphasis mine), using all plural verbs as well. The emphasis is on the unity of God's creation of one diverse humanity, in which every human individually and all humans corporately are God's image bearers. The interplay between humanity as singular (a unified whole) and as plural (individuals interdependent on one another) continues in Genesis 2.

What Does It Mean to Be God's Image?

The scholarship behind our understanding of the "image of God" has existed for decades, but only recently has it begun to reach the wider public.

When asked what my favorite book is, I often respond that it's the published version of a Harvard dissertation written by Catherine McDowell, *The Image of God in the Garden of Eden.*[18] Learning about the image of God was transformative in my life. As a biblical interpreter, I seek to understand what the original authors of the biblical text were saying. McDowell, along with many other scholars such as Carmen Imes, demonstrates that ancient Egypt, Mesopotamia, and Israel had common understandings for the meaning of image and likeness, which sheds light on this concept for us today.

The societies surrounding Israel all made idols, or statues, of their gods out of stone, clay, bronze, or precious metals. After the idol was formed, it was often taken to a garden or by a stream to complete a vivification process to bring life into the idol.

One common set of rituals performed on idols in Mesopotamia and Egypt was called the Washing of the Mouth and the Opening of the Mouth ceremony, giving the god the ability to speak. A final procedure was the Opening of the Eyes ceremony. When the mouth and the eyes of the statue were opened, it would be inhabited by a spiritual entity, making it a god. We recognize the use of this language in Genesis 3. The serpent says, "When you eat from it your eyes will be opened, and you will be like God [or gods], knowing good and evil" (Gen 3:5). This leads us to understand that the actual desire of the man and the woman was *to become a god* on their own. The temptation they quickly yielded to was to no longer be reliant on God but to be the arbitrators of good and bad for themselves, independent of God.

Outside of Israel, statues were also made of kings or governors of their lands, who were generally considered gods themselves, or at least the representative of one of the gods of their land. These statues were physical images of the leader's essence and also stood for their government. Therefore, the statues made in their image and likeness were to be treated with the same level of respect as the leader himself, or herself. For example, some of the best known are the statues of Ramesses II. Many of the statues of the pharaohs still stand at the entryways, temples, and walled cities of Egypt. Statues of other kings were similarly placed, like the statue of the ruler Hadad-yith'i at Tell Fekheriye in northern Syria. The inscription on his statue uses the same ancient words, describing the statue as the "image and likeness" of the governor, as in Genesis 1:26, where humanity is the image and likeness of God.[19]

The inscriptions often found at the base of these statues first give a dedication to the king's or governor's ruling god. After this tribute are statements along the line of "This is the image of king (or governor) such and such. This image represents the king himself and his government. The way you treat this image is just like the way you treat the king himself. Therefore, if you treat this image well and respect it, you are giving respect to the king." A list of blessings follows. "But if you do any damage to this statue, if you mar the statue or treat it badly, it's like you are doing that to the king himself." After the list of blessings is a list of curses that will come upon anyone who dares mistreat the statue.

In the Old Testament, the word "image" or "statue" (*tselem*) generally refers to an illicit idol that God prohibits. Therefore, McDowell notes that "an explicitly positive or favorable meaning of *tselem* occurs only when it describes the creation of mankind."[20] Daniel Fleming helpfully points out, "Read in light of the Bible's abhorrence of images, Gen 1:26 proposes that humanity itself, male and female, represent the only acceptable statues of God. The only legitimate representation of the Creator has been made by himself."[21]

The big contrast between the creation of humans in the Bible and the creation of humans in the rest of the ancient Near East is that outside of the Bible, only kings and rulers were divine image bearers (or some were considered gods themselves). The rest of the masses were created by the gods to serve the gods and their appointed rulers: to bring them food, build them temples, fight their wars, etc. Humans were considered noisy and annoying. In contrast, in Genesis and throughout the rest of the Bible, every human being is God's image bearer. Every human bears the dignity and value of God himself. God takes personally the way we treat every other human being, including ourselves.

Image language from Genesis 1 onward is kinship, family language. It is also royalty language. For we are made in God's image *so that* we may rule. The intended purpose for every human is to be royal children of God. We are created to be God's representatives, carrying out his blessings, bringing his goodness, and fighting against the wrongs and injustices in the world.

In Genesis, the fall did not cause humans to lose their status as divine image bearers. For in Genesis 5:1–3, image-of-God language returns and continues through the human genealogy: "This is the record of the generations of Adam. When God created

Adam, he made him in the likeness of God. Male and female he created them. And he blessed them. And he called their name 'Humankind' when they were created. And when Adam had lived one hundred thirty years, he fathered of a child in his likeness, according to his image. And he called his name Seth" (LEB).

Just as humans did not lose their status as image bearers after the fall, neither did humans lose their status as divine image bearers after the flood. For in Genesis 9:5–7, God requires every human to give account for the way they treat every other human being *because* "in his own image God made humankind." And God repeats the creation blessing he first spoke in Genesis 1:28. God never stops taking personally the way every human treats any another human, *especially* the way people in positions of power or influence treat others. We hear this throughout the words of the psalmists and the prophets. And we hear this in the words of Jesus, who points out that God's rulership is in stark contrast to human rulership, saying, "You know that the rulers of the Gentiles lord it over them, and their high officials exercise authority over them. Not so with you. Instead, whoever wants to become great among you must be your servant," (Matt 20:25–26 NIV). Furthermore, Jesus tells us that he takes personally the way we treat every other human being: "The King will reply, 'Truly I tell you, whatever you did for one of the least of these brothers and sisters of mine, you did for me. . . . Whatever you did not do for one of the least of these, you did not do for me.'" (Matt 25:40, 45 NIV).

God elevates every human being no matter how marred or broken and expects us to do the same. God's plan from the beginning has never changed. Who we are and who God expects us to be in this physical universe sets the foundation for how we view and treat every person, man and woman. Any reading of Scripture that twists this truth corrupts the mission of God, which he declared from the beginning as "very good."

Reflect on the Chapter

* What does the creation account in Genesis reveal about who God is?
* What does the creation account reveal about the value of humanity to God?
* How does the creation account in Genesis differ from other Near Eastern stories of the creation of the world and humans?

Reflect on Your Life

* Identify some specific ways in which God made you in his image.
* How does knowing that every human bears the dignity and value of God himself affect how you see yourself and value others?

Take Your Bold Step

* God elevates every human being no matter how marred or broken and expects us to do the same. Take a moment to think of someone who is being mistreated, and ask God to reveal what you can do to help restore their dignity, such as speaking up for them in a meeting, promoting policy changes at your school or workplace, or partnering with an advocacy or humanitarian aid group.
* Pray for someone who does not know their value to God. Share with them that they are made in God's image and have infinite worth to him.

Breath Prayer

(Inhale)   Our Creator God,

(Exhale)   thank you for making me in your image.

CHAPTER 2

Man and Woman as Sacred Space

GENESIS 2

Humanity is intended to represent God as his royal priestly family on the physical earth. Genesis 2 gives us pictures in story form to help us know how to live together as his divine representatives and carriers of his presence.

Our identity and purpose as God's image bearers in Genesis 1 continue to take shape in Genesis 2. Here we see God's personal touch as he forms the earthling (the *adam*) with dust from the earth (the *adamah*, Gen 2:7). With the closeness of a kiss, the Lord God breathes divine life into his nostrils, and the person becomes a living being. The fusion of soil and Spirit points to our inherent contradictions. We are dust and divinity. Little wonder we feel pulled in two directions—earthbound and heavenward.

The narrative expands in intricate imagery to help us imagine life in the garden and to show what life is like when people are rightly aligned with God and one another. Genesis 2:4–25 instructs us about our essence, identity, and mission. This passage reveals powerful insights, building on the dignity of all people as God's coregents. But some poor translations obscure God's beautiful picture, minimizing or degrading the importance of humanity in general and women in particular. Wrong concepts from these faulty translations are then taught as authoritative truth. I won't speak to the motives of the translators or preachers but rather point to the uplifting and biblically solid correctives.

Four Key Attributes of Our Identity in Genesis 2

Four key attributes serve as a blueprint for our identity and our purpose as humanity.

HUMAN IDENTITY

God made one humanity with diversity. As Genesis 1:27 (NRSVA) states, "So God created humankind in his image, in the image of God he created them [singular in the Hebrew]; male and female he created them [plural in the Hebrew]." In the Septuagint (the Greek translation of the Hebrew Bible), humankind is *ton anthrōpon*, from the Greek root word *anthrōpos*. This word is not distinctly male, but rather, is the word for "humanity" or "human being," which includes males and females.

Likewise, in Genesis 2:7, the Septuagint rightly translates the Hebrew word *adam* as *ton anthrōpon*, "the human being." For there is one humanity—not separate creations of man and woman. We are of one substance together. Since *adam* (humanity) was taken from the *adamah* (the earth), what humanity does impacts the earth itself. The emphasis is on the unity of humanity with God, with the earth, and with one another.

Humanity (*adam*) in Genesis 1:27 and 2:7 refers to man and woman, together. These passages about male and female in Genesis aren't intended as biology lessons, but lessons in anthropology, teaching us what *kind* of being God created us to be. They don't explain *how* God made one humanity in two parts, but rather that humanity will rightly represent God in the world only as one humankind comprised of males and females. The unity in diversity functioning together as God's representatives is key.

It also obliterates any separation by racial or ethnic divides. All such human power-driven distinctions deface the image of God.

The diversification of the *adam* as male and female is important to human identity.[1] The first basic kinship set for human identity is male and female. The man voices this realization when he is introduced to the woman as the other half of his wholeness, expressed in poetic form: "This is now bone of my bones and flesh of my flesh" (Gen 2:23). The composite term "flesh and bone" in both the Old Testament and the New Testament consistently refers to a kinship relationship, to family.[2] Perhaps God placed a pause between the need for companionship and the provision because he wanted the man to feel the lack of his other half so he would appreciate the wholeness the woman brings him. We cannot truly know ourselves as individuals without knowing ourselves in relationship with others, especially those who are different from us.[3]

MORAL IDENTITY

God's prescription to eat from *every tree* of the garden, with the prohibition against eating from *one tree*, gives humanity the opportunity to learn about moral character (Gen 2:16–17). This is unique to humans as earthly creatures. Jacqueline Lapsley points out that before humans are given the right to choose between all the trees in the garden or the Tree of the Knowledge of Good and Evil, "the *adam* is without a moral identity, in the sense that without any prohibitions of any kind, no moral decision making is expected or required of the human being."[4]

It's important to note that the first "command"[5] God gives in the Bible is a positive one: "The LORD God commanded the human, saying 'From every tree of the Garden, Eat freely!'" (Gen 2:16, my translation). Or, as I like to elaborate from the context of Genesis 2:9, "Look at all the beautiful and delicious trees I made for you! Enjoy them all!"

The second command establishes a moral-ethical boundary: "There is something off-limits for you, even though you're in my image and therefore it is available to you. You have the ability, the right, to choose independence from me and to decide for yourselves what is good or bad, right or wrong, in the world I have given you authority over as stewards. But if you decide to go against my wisdom, the consequences will bring chaos and death instead of harmony and life" (my expanded living translation of Gen 2:17).

At this point in the narrative, choice has become "a meaningful category."[6] Baird Callicott explains further that moral choice entails "the power to *judge*, to *decide*, to *determine* what is right and what is wrong *in relation to self*."[7] Once aware of the power of choice, "human beings became conscious of their capacity for good as well as evil."[8] The decision that the man and the woman make in the next chapter is not based on God's perspective of what is good, but rather on what they themselves perceive as beneficial for the *self* rather than for the good of the *other.*

The man and the woman are allowed to make mistakes and receive the consequences for their decisions.

Priestly Identity

Eden is not only a lavish garden but also a sanctuary, a replica of the heavenly temple. A temple is where God makes his presence known on the earth.[9] The tabernacle and Solomon's Temple were patterned after the garden and the heavenly temple. God dwelled in the garden, close to the first man and woman.[10] In light of Genesis 1:26–28, God's image bearers were to represent and reflect God's goodness in such a way that his glorious presence, initially limited to the garden temple of Eden, was to be extended throughout the whole earth.[11] What an amazing vision! God never gives up on this vision. Jesus renews this vision as the goal of the church—God's people rightly representing him as we follow Jesus.

While on earth, Jesus describes himself incarnate as the temple (John 2:21); he was the place where the presence of God dwelled on earth. After Jesus ascends to heaven, he sends the Holy Spirit to dwell in us. Our bodies are now temples of the Holy Spirit (1 Cor 3:16; 6:19). And in Christ, God's people are collectively his temple: "In him the whole structure is joined together and grows into a holy temple in the Lord, in whom you also are built together spiritually into a dwelling place for God" (Eph 2:21–22 NRSVue).

Finally, when Jesus returns, the whole earth will be redeemed and in effect be a sanctuary where God will dwell among the people and sit upon the throne (Revelation 21–22).[12]

This is God's plan in the beginning, where both the garden and the people are God's beautiful and holy temple. God installs the humans into this sacred space and instills them with purpose.[13] The passage reads, "And the LORD God took the *adam* and installed him in the garden of Eden to serve it and to protect it" (Gen 2:15, my translation). Two of the verbs used in Genesis 2:15, "serve and protect" are only paired together in the Hebrew Bible when referring to "'serving and guarding / obeying' God's word," or "to priests who 'serve' God in the temple and 'guard' the sanctity and the purity of the temple (Num 3:7–8; 8:25–26; 18:5–6; 1 Chr 23:32; Ezek 44:14)."[14]

The humans (man and woman together) are to serve and protect the garden as sacred space, a place where God could abide with humans. This divine assignment, however, foreshadows the possibility of a threat to the garden and speaks to humanity's responsibility to protect the sanctity of the place. The *adam* is told to be alert because malevolent spiritual forces had already rebelled against God.

Therefore, after installing the human in the garden temple, giving purpose and boundaries, the Lord God says that it's not good for the *adam* to be alone. However, in the next sentences in

Genesis 2:18–23, a few key Hebrew words poorly translated into English have harmed our understanding of women as co–image bearers of God.

IDENTITY AS FEMALE AND MALE: MAN AND WOMAN AS SACRED SPACE

In the beautiful garden sanctuary, one thing is not good. It isn't evil, but it is *not good*. It is not good for the man to be alone. Life in the garden isn't only to relax and enjoy the good food. As a priest, the human is also supposed to be on guard duty, protecting the sacred space. For this, the human needs a strong partner.

Genesis 2:18–23 is intended to help us understand how we are to relate to one another as male and female. Tragically, the insufficient translations along with poor teaching have led to marred relationships and a confused image of God. Here's the passage with a few troubled translations in bold that have led to confusion and bad behavior:

> Then the LORD God said, "It is not good that the man should be alone; I will make him a **helper** [*ezer*] as his partner." So out of the ground the LORD God formed every animal of the field and every bird of the air, and brought them to the man to see what he would call them; and whatever the man called every living creature, that was its name. The man gave names to all cattle, and to the birds of the air, and to every animal of the field; but for the man there was not found a **helper** [*ezer*] as his partner.
>
> So the LORD God caused a deep sleep to fall upon the man, and he slept; then he took one of his **ribs** [*tsela*] and closed up its place with flesh. And the **rib** [*tsela*] that the LORD God had taken from the man **he made** [*bnh*, built] into a woman and brought her to the man. Then the man said,

"This at last is bone of my bones
and flesh of my flesh;
this one shall be called Woman,
for out of Man this one was taken." (NRSVue)

We'll look at the words in bold to get a better understanding of God's intentions for humans as male and female.

Ezer: A Strong Partner

Quite a lot has been written about this Hebrew word *ezer* in scholarship and for the broader public.[15] The word *ezer* occurs in Genesis 2:18 and 20. Most of the major English translations render *ezer* as "helper, help," except a few that render it "companion" (MSG, TLB, NET). When I teach these verses, I ask the students what words or images they associate with "helper" in Genesis 2. Inevitably, I'm told, "assistant," "housekeeper," "secretary," etc.; characters from the movie *The Help*; or some other person of lesser position or authority giving aid to someone of greater position.

However, *ezer* occurs twenty-one times in the Hebrew Bible, twice here in Genesis and nineteen times elsewhere—predominantly in military contexts.[16] In sixteen of the twenty-one occurrences, *ezer* refers to the Lord God as our help! We can be sure that God is not anyone's assistant, doing our dishes or cleaning up after us.

Here are a few examples of the Lord as *ezer*:[17]

1. Exodus 18:4: Moses named his son Eliezer, for he said, "My father's God was my helper; he saved me from the sword of Pharaoh."
2. Psalm 20:2 (NRSVue): "May he [the Lord] send you help from the sanctuary and give you support from Zion."

3. Psalm 115:9: "All you Israelites, trust in the LORD—he is their help and shield."
4. Psalm 124:8 (NRSVue): "Our help is in the name of the LORD, who made heaven and earth."

Although the translations also use "help" or "helper" for God, *ezer* has developed a very different connotation in Genesis 2 when referring to women. From the Hebrew use of the word *ezer*, woman should be understood as a divine help, a strong ally serving and protecting with the man as priests in the garden. Yet so few English translations have changed their rendering of the Hebrew *ezer* in Genesis 2:18 and 20. This has led to ineffectiveness in our mutual work in the church and in the world.

Unfortunately, in the garden, neither the man nor woman resist the serpent's temptation to be their own god. But God's divine assignment remains. As the continuing story of Scripture shows, many women do step boldly into their role as *ezer*! This significant God-given identity is lived out by the women in the following chapters, demonstrating what has too often been missed.

Tsela: Holding Up Our Side of Sacred Space

Genesis 2 gives us a second image to further help us understand man and woman's role in the world as God's image bearer. The Lord God gives us another perhaps even more vibrant image of his plan for how man and woman are to represent him in the world through the Hebrew word *tsela*, which is almost always mistranslated into English as "rib" in Genesis 2:21–22. As some prominent but ignored scholars have pointed out, it should be translated "side."[18]

The Hebrew word *tsela* occurs forty times in the Hebrew Bible. The only place it is translated "rib" is in Genesis 2:21–22. Every major English Bible since the 1530 Tyndale version translates *tsela* as "rib," except the NET Bible and the Amplified Bible ("part he had taken out of the man," "part"). The passage reads, "And the Lord God built from the side which he took from the *adam* into a woman, and he brought her to the *adam*" (my translation).

Centuries of mistranslation and misconceptions need to be corrected because Genesis 1–3 is "the very base of Western perception of femininity."[19] Comments about women as Adam's rib have generally been negative and sometimes deplorable with slurs regarding the inferior or backbiting character of women.[20] As Anne Lerner observes, "The creation of the first woman has been viewed as secondary to the man's; her substance, derivative; her eating the fruit of the forbidden tree, culpable; her status relative to her man, subordinate. Her story, framed by her creation from a rib and by her banishment from the Garden of Eden, has been exploited to validate the dependent, circumscribed position of women."[21]

Wilda Gafney notes, "The *tzela'* [or *tsela*] that God removes is a 'side' and not a 'rib' as commonly mistranslated. Throughout Exodus the *tzela'* of the ark of the covenant on which its poles are alternately set are its sides. There is no other place in Scripture in which *tzela'* is translated as a rib."[22] Let's look more closely at the word *tsela* and why I and other scholars call "rib" a mistranslation.

Outside of Genesis 2:21–22, *tsela* is never translated "rib." It is almost always translated "side." And it's not just any word for side. It has a unique and special use. Other than the two translations as "rib" in Genesis 2:21–22, all but two uses of *tsela* are special architectural terms for the sides of sacred places where God makes his presence known:

- Side walls / chambers of the temple, which are structurally necessary for the temple to stand[23] — fifteen times, 1 Kgs 6:5, 8, 15 (2x), Ezek 41:5, 6 (4x), 7, 8, 9 (2x), 11, 26
- Sides to the entrance (nave / side doors) of the temple — one time, 1 Kgs 6:34

- Side walls of the holy of holies — one time, 1 Kgs 6:16
- Sides of the tabernacle — seven times; Exod 26:20, 26, 27 (2x); 36:25, 31, 32
- Sides of the ark of the covenant–holding up the mercy seat — eight times, Exod 25:12 (2x), 14; 26:35 (2x); 37:3 (2x), 5
- Sides of the altar of incense — two times, Exod 30:4; 37:27
- Sides of the altar of burnt offering — two times, Exod 27:7; 38:7
- Side beams of Solomon's house — one time; *not* sacred space: 1 Kgs 7
- Side of the hill where Shimei threw stones at David as he left Jerusalem when Absalom took his throne — one time, *not* sacred space, 2 Sam 16:13

All but the last two are holy places. The sides of each of these structures must be present, of equivalent size and shape, and capable of bearing the weight of the lid or the roof.* If one of the sides were missing, deficient, or wobbly, the temple would collapse, the tabernacle would not stand, the mercy seat would not rest upon the ark of the covenant, and the incense that represents the prayers of God's people and the sacrifices to God upon the altar could not be offered.

---

* There are at least eight other words for "side" in the Hebrew Bible. Each of these other words have many different uses but are not substituted for *tsela*. For example, one common Hebrew word, *tsad*, is used to refer to one side of Noah's ark for the door (Gen 6:16); people as thorns in the Israelite's side (Num 33:55; Jos 23:13); Ezekiel lying on one side (Ezek 4:4). Another Hebrew word, *ever*, generally refers to "side" as a territorial edge, such as the sides of a hill (1 Sam 26:13); one side of a city (1 Kings 4:12); or the sides of a river (Deut 30:13). In contrast, *tsela* is not used anywhere in the Hebrew Bible to refer to a human body part. Much later, *tsela* began to be used figuratively for ribs. A similar Aramaic word occurs in Daniel 3:5, and possibly in Hebrew in the apocryphal book of Jubilees 3:5; both of these texts are from around the 2nd century BC. However, "The idea that Eve was made out of one of Adam's ribs has its origin in rabbinical lore," which ranges from the second to the seventh century AD, many more centuries after the Hebrew Bible was complete.

The understanding we gain from this imagery is that both man and woman are necessary to take their stand as holy sides for God's presence and power to be manifested in the earthly realm. Woman and man are essential as the sides of the frame, opposite to the other, upholding the image of God together as one unit. If woman is beat down or excluded, or if man tries to take both sides in God's spiritual architecture, sacred space is left in shambles. God's work and presence will not be manifested.

Therefore, the *Theological Dictionary of the Old Testament*, a prominent Hebrew lexicon (dictionary), concludes, "Given the fact that *tsela* is seen as meaning 'rib' only in the context of the creation of woman, it is unlikely that it is a correct reading."[24] Other prominent scholars agree with that conclusion.[25] Additional textual support for the allusion to the sanctuary is "its association in Genesis 2 with the verb *banah*; 'build, architecturally design.' . . . Thus the 'rib / side' used by the Lord as the basis for the 'building' of Eve is another of the numerous hints or echoes of the tabernacle/Temple."[26] Man and woman are "creative co-participants, spiritual intimates, yes, priests, in the sacred worship service of the Eden sanctuary."[27]

Conclusion

Genesis 2 expands our sacred imaginations to see God's vision for humanity united in our diversity as divine image bearers with moral and priestly identities as male and female. Without a proper understanding of how God made woman as *ezer* and *tsela*, neither men nor women can fulfill their God-given purpose. If, however, women and men partner together and support one another in our human, moral, and priestly identities, we will manifest God's presence and glory to a broken world in need of healing and redemption.

Reflect on the Chapter

* What did you learn about human, moral, priestly, or female identity in Genesis 2?
* How does knowing that the word *ezer* in Scripture typically refers to God's help or God as our helper shape your view of how God created woman to be an *ezer* (Gen 2:18)?
* Outside of Genesis 2, what does the word *tsela* refer to in Scripture? How does that impact your understanding of God's plan for the relationship between man and woman and their sacred joint purpose?

Reflect on Your Life

* Dr. Faro writes, "If woman is beat down or excluded, or if man tries to take both sides in God's spiritual architecture, sacred space is left in shambles." If you have experienced or observed this, describe how that affected your life, church, or community.
* Conversely, in what ways have you seen men and women partnering together in unity that make God's presence and power known (not just in a marriage relationship)?

Take Your Bold Step

* Consider a few concrete ways you want to grow in being an *ezer* (not limited to the context of marriage), such as providing leadership when challenges arise, mentoring and empowering others, using your voice to speak out against injustice, and building strong relationships of support.
* How can you encourage, champion, or equip women in your sphere so that they can live out God's plan for them as *ezers* in their lives? Some examples include mentoring

them so they can develop their unique gifts, connecting them to new people, and giving them opportunities to lead.

Breath Prayer

(Inhale)   Thank you, God,

(Exhale)   for your presence dwelling in us.

CHAPTER 3

Redemption Hope
Through the Woman

GENESIS 3—4

G od's beautiful vision of his intentions for life on this earth
is presented to us in Genesis 2. Life is as it should be: abun-
dant, harmonious, peaceful, very good. The "not good" of human
isolation finds fulfillment in community. Man rejoices when
woman enters the scene. The first recorded human words in the
Bible are Adam's poetic exuberance toward his strong ally who is
"At last!" with him: "The man said, 'This is now bone of my bones
and flesh of my flesh; she shall be called "woman," for she was
taken out of man'" (Gen 2:23 NTL, NIV). "The self, the 'I,' discovers
itself in greeting another."[1]

Woman is one substance with man. Yet they are not the same.
But in their separateness, they are one (Gen 2:23–24). Their union
is grounded in trust, expressed by the words, "Adam and his wife
were both naked, and they felt no shame" (Gen 2:25). They are
fully disclosed before each other with no hidden motives. Life is
whole.

Eve in Hebrew means "the mother of all living." Although the
woman was drawn from the *adam*, every human being thereafter
is drawn from a woman. Man and woman are inexorably intertwined in their being and becoming.

Alienation from God and Each Other

Genesis 3 and 4 reveal how the harmony of the garden falls apart. But God does not leave us without hope. The degradation of human relationships begins with believing a lie. The serpent twists God's words, implying that God has lied and is withholding goodness from them (Gen 3:1–4). In falling prey to this falsehood, Adam and Eve *take* what now appears desirable: independence from God (Gen 3:5–6). This independence separates them from each other and their interconnectedness with creation.

In their new state of self-deification, they recognize their vulnerability, feel a new sensation—*fear*—and scramble to hide (Gen 3:7, 10). Along with fear comes shame, which produces blame: the man refuses to take responsibility for his actions, casting his shadow on God and the woman. The vilification of women has persisted ever since Adam tried to throw the blame for his mutiny off himself.

However, Adam is present during the whole dark conversation with the serpent. Although the serpent is addressing the woman, he speaks to both of them using the plural *you* verbs: "Did God really say, 'You [plural] must not eat from any tree in the garden'?" as in "the both of you," which is evident in the Hebrew (Gen 3:1, 4, 5). Furthermore, the biblical text says that the man was right there. He was "with her," and she was "with me" (Gen 3:6, 12). Both were complicit in the decision to eat from the forbidden tree.

They both fail their priestly assignment to *serve* and *protect* the garden, their sacred home (Gen 2:15). They both believe the serpent's lies more than what God has spoken and act on their desire to be gods, to their mutual demise.

The Lord God speaks first to the man because God had first directly spoken to him when he gave instructions regarding the Tree. The problem was *not* that the man listened to the woman but that he failed to obey God's clear command. God does not let the man off the hook but asks him, "Who told you that you were naked? Have you eaten from the tree that I commanded you not to eat from?" (Gen 3:11).[2] God holds the man accountable for his actions, just as he holds the woman responsible for hers.

The last words of Adam recorded in Scripture are, "The woman you put here with me—she gave me some fruit from the tree, and I ate it" (Gen 3:12). He expresses no remorse. Instead, he blames God: "The woman you put here with me"! His words expose his treason against the heavenly realm, blaming God foremost and secondly blaming the woman for his actions.

Many male commentators on this passage throughout history have continued the secondary sin of Adam, shifting the blame to Eve in particular and extend Eve's sin to label all women as seducers of men, shifting the culpability for their own wrongful actions onto women. If these analysts and preachers were truthful, they would realize they are blaming God, who made women along with men in his image and deemed his creation "very good" (Gen 1:26–28, 31).

God then turns to the woman and asks, "What is this you have done?" (Gen 3:13). The woman is not accountable for the man's sin. And as Carmen Joy Imes observes, "God does not hold Adam accountable for Eve's sin; she possesses her own dignity as a moral agent. God's question gives her an opportunity to confess: 'The serpent deceived me, and I ate' (Gen. 3:13)."[3] Although both the man and the woman transgressed God's command, the woman's statement is accurate (Gen 2:16–17; 1 Tim 2:14).

As Katharine Bushnell notes, "Eve's answer to God was better than Adam's. Adam casts aspersions on God for giving him Eve, referring to her as 'the woman you put here with me' (v. 12). It's easy for us also to point the finger at Eve, blaming her for the human predicament, the path of sin we all have chosen. Eve instead correctly identifies the serpent as the tempter and herself as the one who made the choice."[4]

The Lord then addresses the serpent. God curses the serpent with a low earthly existence (3:14). Please notice a common misconception: The snake is cursed, but the woman and the man are not! The woman and the man experience consequences for their choices, but God does not say they are cursed (vv. 16–19). The ground also is cursed because of humans separating themselves from God and separating themselves from his assignment to them as stewards of his creation.

God then pronounces the consequences for the serpent's actions: the ensuing conflict between the serpent and the woman, with the promise of redemption from the serpent's bite through the woman and her offspring, literally "her seed."

> And I will put enmity
>> between you and the woman,
>> and between your offspring [seed] and hers;
> he will crush your head,
>> and you will strike [crush] his heel. (Gen 3:15)

We'll return to this hope shortly. But first, God pronounces the cost of the woman's and the man's betrayal.

Broken Relationships, Grief, and Hardship

Tim Mackie of the BibleProject calls these pronouncements on the woman and the man "God's lament": "Yahweh naming the new normal in light of the decisions that they have made."[5] The consequences for what each has done are closely related and share some common language.[6] Genesis 3:16 states,

> To the woman he said,

"I will greatly multiply your hardship [*itsavon*] and
   conception.
   In grief [*etsev*] you will bring forth children."
   (my translation)

Our English translations wrongly say that women will experience increased pain during childbirth or labor. The three Hebrew
words used throughout the Old Testament for labor pains or
childbirth are not used here.* Rather, as Iain Provan points out,
"Gen 3:16 refers to the 'agony, hardship, worry, and anxiety' of the
circumstances in which children are conceived, born, and raised,
and in which they die."[7]

In Genesis 3:17, the Lord God tells the man the consequences
of his action:

"Cursed is the ground because of you;
   through hardship [*itsavon*] you will eat food
      from it
   all the days of your life." (my translation)

Notice that the word *itsavon*, meaning grief and "mental
anguish," is the same in verses 16 and 17.[8] Both man and woman
suffer grief in their pursuits of love and fruitfulness. In the home,
the woman "suffers pain (*itsavon*) . . . not only because she is in
conflict with the man, but also because the man is in conflict
with the earth, and the entire community suffers as a result."[9]

Not only do man and woman suffer grief due to their actions,
God also experiences grief in his heart due to the corruption and

---

*   The three Hebrew words that refer specifically to labor pain are צרר (*ṣrr* in the *hiph*,
Jer 48:41; 49:22), חבל (*ḥbl* in the piel, Ps 7:15; Song 8:5), and חול (*ḥwll*); see in particular
Provan, "Pain in Childbirth?," 287–94, who demonstrates through extensive exegesis of
this passage that the Hebrew word used here (*herôn*, from the verb *hārâ*) refers specifically to being/becoming pregnant and nowhere to labor pains or giving birth.

evil that humanity inflicts on his good creation. The verb (*'tsb*) that describes God's grief in Genesis 6:6, leading up to the flood, comes from the same word that speaks of the pain and anguish suffered by the woman and man in Genesis 3:16–17 (*itsavon*). All uses of this root word (*etsev* and *itsavon*) speak of the pain and sorrows experienced by humanity due to life conditions after the garden.[10]

The family stories in Genesis continue this trajectory. Children are conceived amid angst, jealousy, and broken relationships. Sarah and Hagar, Ishmael and Isaac, Esau and Jacob, and Rachel and Leah all provide vivid stories of dysfunctional life in exile from Eden. Each family undergoes the test of believing God or not. Sarah, Rebecca, and Rachel struggle with infertility, which parallels Abraham's and Isaac's struggles with famine, when they're willing to give away their wives for their own personal safety and profit.[11]

The consequences of our determination to live independently from God are demonstrated in our innate longing to experience fruitfulness and multiplication in our various domains of life. But our efforts are fraught with grief, hardship, striving, and loss when man and woman each seeks to control their environment while refusing to yield control to God Almighty.

Eve Speaks the First Words of Hope After the Exile

Eve experiences the consequences of her disobedience, including grief and dysfunction, but she does not let that paralyze her. She actively anticipates One who will be born through her, a seed who will crush the head of the serpent. The hope of promise is first echoed in her strange words.[12] Genesis 4 begins, "Now Adam knew Eve his wife, and she conceived and gave birth to Cain. And she said, 'I have acquired [*qnh*] a man [*ish*] with Yahweh.'

Then she gave birth again to his brother Abel" (Gen 4:1–2a, my translation).

The language of this birthing narrative is highly unusual. There is no other parallel in Scripture.[13] A leading dictionary of biblical Hebrew rightly uses "uncertain" to describe the meaning of this verse.[14] Adam is not given credit for the child. Eve's covenant God, Yahweh, is. Let's look closely at her words.

She names her son Cain, which comes from the word often translated "acquired" (*qanah* or *qnh,* in Hebrew). Scholars disagree on the translation for this verb that Eve uses. It can mean "to buy, acquire, or produce," but a similar form of this word can mean "create."[15] The Septuagint (ancient Greek) translation maintains the ambiguity of her words, that she "acquired a man through [via] God."[16]

Furthermore, she doesn't call her newborn a baby or a boy but a man, an *ish.* Her language echoes Adam's exuberant words when he first saw her and called her *ishah* in Genesis 2:23. "Eve now says, in effect: 'I, a woman (*ishah*), was produced from man (*ish*); now I, woman, have in turn produced a man.'"[17]

She declares that this man she bore was acquired not with Adam but with Yahweh, which can imply "together with" the Lord. There is ambiguity concerning the meaning of the little word *'et* that connects man (*ish*) *with* the Lord (Yahweh). This word *'et* can either mean "with" as in, "I have gained a man with the Lord," or it can be a direct object marker, as in, "I have gained a man, the Lord."[18] Some, such as Martin Luther, understand her statement as a declaration of faith in the messianic promise from Genesis 3:15.

Regardless of how her curious words are understood, Scripture notes that the sacred covenant name of Yahweh was first uttered by the woman, Eve.[19] And she is the first to give God glory after their exile from the garden.

Eve's Final Words and the Hope of Redemption

Yet for all Eve's expectations, her hope for Cain is dashed when he murders her son Abel. Despite what must have been overwhelming grief to lose a son at the hands of another son, Eve still has faith that God will fulfill his promise. She speaks yet once more toward the close of this chapter in Genesis, initiating language that becomes synonymous with salvation: "Then Adam knew his wife again, and she gave birth to a son. And she called his name Seth [*shet*], for [she said], 'God has appointed [*shyt*] to me another seed [*zera'*] in place of Abel, because Cain killed him.' And as for Seth, he also fathered a son, and he called his name Enosh. At that time people began to call on the name of Yahweh" (Gen 4:25–26, my translation). The name Seth comes from the verb *shyt* that was used in Genesis 3:15 and designates him as the hopefully promised seed who will crush the head of the serpent.

Through the sorrow of events and the passage of time, Eve credits God for the birth of her son Seth, the appointed seed. Here is where these two key words in Hebrew previously occurred together only in Genesis 3:15:

> And I will put [*shyt*] enmity
>> between you and the woman,
>> and between your offspring [*zera'*] and hers;
> he will crush your head,
>> and you will strike his heel.

Eve demonstrates her continued faith in Yahweh's promise by directly connecting his promise in Genesis 3:15 with the name she gives her son Seth. Furthermore, the narrative points to the fruit of her faith in the verse that follows: "Seth also had a son, and he named him Enosh. At that time people began to call on the name of the LORD" (Gen 4:26).

Seth's son, whom he names Enosh, means "mortal." *Enosh* becomes a word for "human" (with an emphasis on our mortality), just as *adam* means human in the rest of the Hebrew Bible.[20] In a genuine sense, Enosh becomes the second Adam, but one aware of our mortality and dependency on Yahweh.[21] Through the line of Seth and Enosh, the Messiah is birthed.

As Abraham Kuyper wrote in 1933, "In her there lay concealed as in a kernel a woman's grace and independence, her susceptibility to Satan, but her susceptibility to the faith as well."[22] Kuyper continues,

> Into the profound soul of this woman God sowed the seeds of a glorious faith, and by means of it again permitted heaven to arise before her. The seed of this tempted woman was once to bruise the head of the Tempter. Eve fixed her whole soul to that promise. In fact, when Cain was born to her she supposed that this child was already the promised seed and she exclaimed, "I have gotten a man from the Lord." . . . The disillusionment which followed upon that hope was bitter when, after some years, the earth imbibed the blood of Abel. Yet, after many epochs the Angels of God acknowledged the seed of this woman in the Child of Mary. The Son of Mary was also Eve's child.[23]

The Rest of the Story

Eve's words regarding Seth as another "seed" are followed by this explosive statement: "At that time people began to call on the name of the LORD" (Gen 4:26). This expression "refers to worshiping the LORD through prayer and sacrifice."[24] And even more, the "name of the LORD" represents not only his name, but all that God has revealed about himself. "To 'call on the name of the LORD' is to worship him according to the whole revealed truth of God."[25]

In addition to worship, calling on the name of the Lord becomes associated with salvation. The prophet Joel prophesies deliverance in the last days, proclaiming, "And everyone who calls on the name of the LORD will be saved" (Joel 2:32). Peter quotes Joel's prophecy in his first sermon on the day of Pentecost (Acts 2:21). And Paul in Romans 10:13 repeats the famous verse again: "Everyone who calls on the name of the Lord will be saved."

These all flow from the conclusion of Genesis 4, which introduces the theme of worship, the promise of the messianic lineage, and the message of salvation. Genesis 5 starts with a genealogy, beginning with God's creation of humanity in his image, Adam, Seth, and Enosh, and proceeds through Noah, whose son Shem would continue the messianic line of hope.[26]

The Legacy of Eve

Interpreters and teachers have often vilified Eve, leading to a distorted image of God and a corrupt treatment of humanity. This loss harms all of us. While Eve did fall for the words of the serpent and eat the forbidden fruit, she also demonstrated her faith by returning to God's words of hope. As Abraham Kuyper wrote, "She fixed her whole soul on that promise," first believing that Cain and then Seth might be the promised "seed" of salvation.

Eve, like many of us, was familiar with the grief and pain of life and of family. She mourns the death of her son Abel and the exile of her firstborn. Yet despite these tremendous losses, she still chooses to put her hope in God's promise.

Although Eve does not live to see God's plan fulfilled in the birth of Jesus, she rejoices in the birth of her grandson Enosh and lives to see people begin worshiping the Lord. Eve, the first person in Scripture to utter the name Yahweh, likely played an important role in teaching the next generation how to call upon the Lord and believe once again in his word.

Reflect on the Chapter

* How did you view Eve before reading this chapter? Has your view of Eve changed after reading this chapter, and if so, how?
* After Adam and Eve sinned, God issued consequences to the man and the woman in Genesis 3:16–19. What is similar about the consequences he gave to each of them?
* In what ways did Eve maintain hope in God's promise despite her grief?

Reflect on Your Life

* In addition to the tremendous grief she felt after Cain killed Abel, Eve may also have felt guilt or shame that she should have done something differently as a mother to prevent the tragedy. What in your life has led to disappointment, grief, guilt, or shame that has threatened to paralyze you?
* Romans 8:1–2 says, "Therefore, there is now no condemnation for those who are in Christ Jesus, because through Christ Jesus the law of the Spirit who gives life has set you free from the law of sin and death." How does Eve's example help you move forward in freedom and hope?

Take Your Bold Step

* Eve was hoping that Cain and then Seth might be the "seed" that God promised. Perhaps you also are waiting for God to fulfill a promise to you. Or maybe you have hopes for your children, your vocation, or your partner that are yet unfulfilled. Take some time to pray over these longings and entrust them to the Lord.
* Eve was the first in Scripture to utter the name Yahweh

and was the first to give God glory after their exile from the garden. Dr. Faro writes that calling on the name of the Lord means to "worship him according to the whole revealed truth of God." Look up some names of God from Scripture and praise God using those specific names. For example, "We praise you for being Immanuel, God with us. Thank you for being with me right now."

Breath Prayer

(Inhale)   God, my Deliverer,
(Exhale)   I put my hope in you.

CHAPTER 4

Sarah Brings Life from Death

GENESIS 11:26–25:11

After Eve, the next key figure who advances God's story of salvation is Sarah. Sarai/Sarah appears more than any other woman in the Bible: fifty-four times in the Old Testament and four times in the New Testament. She exhibits faith and failure, like every other key person in this grand story. By his grace, God weaves even the worst parts of people's behaviors into his big picture when they return to him again and again in humble faith.

While Abraham is rightly called the father of our faith,[1] we often miss that the promises would not have been fulfilled without Sarah. As Eve is the mother of all the living, Sarah is the mother of our faith. Sarai means "my princess." Sarah is generally taken to mean "princess of Yahweh." She is his royal daughter.

God's Promises for Abraham and Sarah

The account of Abraham and Sarah (originally Abram and Sarai) starts when a group of people in Shinar of Mesopotamia begins an insurrection against God by constructing the Tower of Babel (Gen 11:1–9). While people of that day were building their own chiefdoms and kingdoms, God reaches out to find those who will hear his voice and follow him. One family in Ur (today, in southern Iraq) responds to God's call and begins their trek to Canaan. They get as far as Harran (today, in southeast Turkey) and settle there, where Abraham's father, Terah, dies (Gen 11:31–32).

In Harran, Abraham hears God's call: "Go from your country, your people and your father's household to the land I will show you" (Gen 12:1). It comes with promises:

> I will make you into a great nation,
>   and I will bless you;
> I will make your name great,
>   and you will be a blessing.
> I will bless those who bless you,
>   and whoever curses you I will curse;
> and all peoples on earth
>   will be blessed through you. (Gen 12:2–3)

Abraham heeds God's call and believes his promises. For nearly twenty-five years, Abraham thinks the promise is about God blessing *him*. He hasn't yet learned that God works through families being faithful to one another and caring for each other. It takes him time to understand that nation-building and God's kind of "power [reside] in the inner workings of the family."[2]

In the church, the promises God gives Abraham are often emphasized and the promises God gives Sarah are overlooked. God told Abraham that he would bless Sarah too, perhaps because Abraham needed to hear Yahweh say this even more than Sarah did. "God also said to Abraham, 'As for Sarai your wife, you are no longer to call her Sarai; her name will be Sarah. I will bless her and will surely give you a son by her. I will bless her so that she will be the mother of nations; kings of peoples will come from her'" (Gen 17:15–16).

God calls Sarah the "mother of nations." Together, Abraham and Sarah are the patriarch and matriarch of the family of faith.

Abraham Disregards Sarah

For most of Sarah's life, however, Abraham didn't seem to value his wife as a copartner in God's promises. We can see this through his words and his actions. When Abraham and Sarah left Harran, he told her, "This is how you can show your love to me: Everywhere we go, say of me, 'He is my brother'" (Gen 20:13), he explains, because "she really is my sister, the daughter of my father though not of my mother; and she became my wife" (v. 12).

Why did he ask Sarah to follow along with his half deception? Abraham himself tells us: "He said to his wife Sarai, 'I know what a beautiful woman you are. When the Egyptians see you, they will say, 'This is his wife.' Then they will kill me but will let you live. Say you are my sister, so that I will be treated well for your sake and my life will be spared because of you'" (Gen 12:11–13; cf. 20:11–12).

Sadly, Abraham lets this happen twice, indicating a lack of concern for his wife's life or safety. He not only exerts no effort to save Sarah but prioritizes protecting his own life and profiting financially. Moreover, Abraham accepts Pharaoh's many gifts when Sarah is taken into his harem (Gen 12:16).

Abraham considers Sarah his trophy wife and dismisses her for his own personal gain. Even after God honors Sarai with her new name of Sarah and tells Abraham that she will give birth to their son of promise and be a mother of nations and kings (Gen 17:15–19), Abraham still exploits her (Gen 20:1–2). But God honors and protects Sarah the second time, from King Abimelek: "for the LORD had kept all the women in Abimelek's household from conceiving *because of Abraham's wife Sarah.* Now the LORD was gracious to Sarah as he had said, and *the LORD did for Sarah as he had promised*" (Gen 20:18–21:1, emphasis mine).

Baruch Levine puts it this way: "Finally, and of major concern, is the emphasis on God's direct, protective intervention—just at the moment when all human resources have failed and it appears that the divine promises are to be aborted. The matriarch is recovered by the action of God, not as a result of warfare waged by the outraged husband."[3]

Abraham twice fails to protect Sarah, trafficking her to the king's harem for personal profit and protection. Yet the New Testament commentary gives witness that Sarah's trust is in God and not in her husband. In these terrible circumstances she put her "hope in God" and refused to "give way to fear" (1 Pet 3:5–6). The Lord protected Sarah's honor (Gen 12:17; 20:16–18).

But Sarah does her share of exploitation also.

Sarah Exploits Hagar

Ten years go by. Although Abraham and Sarah are materially blessed, they have no child, own no land, and haven't been a blessing to the nations around them. Things didn't go too well in Egypt, though they were given more material possessions and slaves.

In ancient cultures, barrenness was a "scandal," as the woman was responsible to bear children for the family's continuation and inheritance. For any woman who couldn't conceive, "taking on a second wife to bear children was a widespread occurrence in the ancient Near East."[4] Because Sarah still has no children, she sees herself as a hindrance to fulfilling God's promises.

Surrogacy, a "borrowed womb," has been practiced in various forms for over four thousand millennia. In ancient times, the wealthy generally forced a slave to have sex with the husband to bear a child on behalf of the first wife, who held claim to the baby in terms of legal rights of motherhood.[5] "Designating a surrogate was a legal action that not only helped the household survive but also preserved the honor of the barren woman."[6]

Scripture doesn't tell us how Abraham and Sarah acquired Hagar. But ironically, since she is identified as an Egyptian, she may have been part of the "property" Pharaoh had given to Abraham (Gen 12:16).

After ten years of trying for a child, Sarah tells Abraham to make use of the culturally acceptable legal provision for barrenness.[7] She says, "The LORD has kept me from having children. Go, sleep with my slave; perhaps I can build a family through her. Abram agreed to what Sarai said" (Gen 16:2).

Although Sarah is legally in her right as the wife to take this initiative, her exploitation of Hagar is no more morally acceptable in God's eyes than Abraham's previous exploitation of Sarah in Egypt. As Tony Maalouf says, "One cannot think of any example involving human exploitation that does not have consequences."[8]

Sarah forces Hagar to have sex with Abraham for the sake of obtaining a legal heir and then severely oppresses Hagar both during her pregnancy and after she gives birth to Ishmael. Once Hagar conceives, Sarah complains to Abraham that Hagar no longer respects her (Gen 16:5 LEB), or "she despises me" (NIV).[9] The behavior of neither woman is right. But even if Sarah is angry or fearful of losing her place, she is by far in the greater wrong for she holds the superior power and, thus, the greater responsibility (Gen 16:5; 21:9–10).

Although Abraham and Sarah know God's promised heir will come through Abraham, it is not until many years after the birth of Ishmael, and twenty-four years after leaving Harran, that the Lord specifies that the promised child will come directly through Sarah (Gen 17:15–16).

Easy as it is to criticize Abraham, Sarah, and Hagar, I can't hold myself superior to any of them by thinking I would have handled their situations any better. The two things that instruct and encourage me, however, are these: God works in the midst of Abraham's and Sarah's flaws, failings, and faith; and God sees Hagar's suffering, reaches out to her, and makes promises to her and Ishmael.

God's Promises to Hagar

Hagar's story illuminates God's love and care for the exploited. She holds a unique place in the Bible. "Hagar receives the first divine annunciation to a woman in the canon of a promised child and promise of a dynasty. Hagar will become the 'Mother of Many Peoples'"[10] (Gen 16:10; 17:20; 21:18). God's promises for Hagar and Ishmael echo the promises to Abraham and Sarah: offspring, blessing, and nations of people.

Hagar is dragged into the drama of Abraham and Sarah's ups and downs, faith and failures, as they try to "help" God fulfill his promises to them. She suffers at their hands. When she is pregnant, she runs away because of Sarah's mistreatment, then returns at God's promise. When Ishmael is about thirteen, she is sent away.

The only fault one can find in Hagar is that when she gets the upper hand, moving from status of slave to pregnant second wife, she taunts Sarah. Sarah, in return, mistreats and oppresses Hagar. What a mess.

But God does not leave Hagar as collateral damage. The Lord steps in, personally pursuing and caring for her. Previously, Sarah, Abraham, and the narrator refer to her only as the slave woman. God is the first one to call her by her name. He then invites her to tell her story: "Hagar . . . where have you come from, and where are you going?" (Gen 16:8). These questions show God's personal interest in her.

Hagar responds in faith and remarkably is the first person in the Bible to give God a name, *El-roi*: "'You are the God who sees me,' for she said, 'I have now seen the One who sees me'" (Gen 16:13).

When she is pregnant and despondent in the wilderness, God hears her cries and assures her, "I will increase your descendants so much that they will be too numerous to count" (Gen 16:10). What's more, he names her son Ishmael, which means "God listens" or "God hears" (Gen 16:11). God named only four people in the Old Testament before they were born: Ishmael, Isaac, Solomon, and Josiah.[11]

Although God tells her to return and "submit under her [Sarai's] hand" (Gen 16:9, my translation), God uses the form of the verb that means to "subject oneself voluntarily" for a season. "Hagar's submission was not asked because God approved of her oppression; it was necessary for his plans."[12] Before, Hagar would have rather died in the desert than bear the cruelty of Sarah, but her encounter with "the God who sees me" gives her the strength to return (Gen 16:13 NIV). The next time Hagar and Ishmael leave (Gen 21:8–21), Ishmael is a circumcised covenant son of Abraham (Gen 17:24–26) and is close to becoming a young man who could care for himself and his mother in the wilderness.

The source of water that God provides for pregnant Hagar in the wilderness is called "*Beer LaHai-Roi*," meaning, the well of the Living One who sees me (Gen 16:14). Curiously, this is where Isaac chooses to live after he is bound as a sacrifice on Mount Moriah (Gen 24:62; 25:9–11). After Abraham dies, Isaac and Ishmael bury him together in the Machpelah cave with Sarah.

Hagar stands out in Scripture as a caring mother and a bold woman of faith who, though oppressed and misused, is pursued by God, trusts in his protection, and believes his promises to her and Ishmael.

Sarah Believes God for Life from Death

In Genesis 17, God tells Abraham that he will bless Ishmael, make him fruitful, and make him into a great nation but specifies that "my covenant I will establish with Isaac, whom Sarah will bear to you by this time next year" (Gen 17:21).[13] Soon after God reveals this to Abraham, the Lord and two other divine messengers appear at his tent. "Then one of them said, 'I will surely return to you about this time next year, and Sarah your wife will have a son.' Now Sarah was listening at the entrance to the tent, which was behind him" (Gen 18:10). This is the first time Sarah hears directly the words that she herself will bear a child. God seems to wait for them to both understand that they are chosen as a couple, as one, so that his promise to make them the parents of nations can be fulfilled.

Abraham and Sarah are already very old, and Sarah is past the age of childbearing. So when she hears these words, Sarah laughs to herself as she thinks, "After I am worn out and my lord is old, will I now have this pleasure?" Then the LORD said to Abraham, "Why did Sarah laugh and say, 'Will I really have a child, now that I am old?' Is anything too hard for the LORD? I will return to you at the appointed time next year, and Sarah will have a son" (Gen 18:12–14).

The words from Genesis 18:14 are generally translated from the Hebrew as, "Is anything too hard for the LORD?" The Septuagint translation (the ancient Greek from around 200 BC) is remarkably close to the words of the angel Gabriel to Mary regarding the birth of Jesus in Luke 1:37:

- "Is anything too marvelous / miraculous for the LORD?" (Gen 18:14, my translation from the Hebrew Masoretic Text).
- "No word from God is without power / impossible" (Gen 18:14, my translation from the Greek Septuagint).
- "No word from God will be without power / impossible" (Luke 1:37, my translation from the Greek Nestle Aland 28).

I believe Mary makes the connection. Certainly, the Jewish readers of Luke did. The similarity between Mary's and Sarah's circumstances is clear.

They are both incapable of conceiving life outside of a miracle of God. In Sarah's case, God waits to speak to her about conceiving life until her womb is dead. Sarah initially laughs at God's promise, but then in God's mercy, he brings her laughter back at the joyous birth of her son. The New Testament commentary states that by faith she "received ability [lit. 'power'] to conceive, even beyond the proper time of life, since she considered Him faithful who had promised" (Heb 11:11–12 NASB; cf. Gen 17:16).

Sarah has faith that God will bring life from the dead, just as Mary has faith that she will conceive as a virgin.

And this is why Sarah is the mother of our faith. Though far from perfect, like the rest of us, she believes God's word. Beyond hope, she trusts God to do what is humanly impossible.

Sarah's Legacy

Sarah believes in God and is a model we can learn from. Like Abraham, she does not do it perfectly! Sarah experiences the consequence of living outside the garden, living in exile in a world hostile toward God and one another: a world of idolatry, violence, and conflict. Like Eve, Sarah experiences grief, pain, and loss in her family circumstances.

Sarah doesn't have perfect faith from beginning to end, but she demonstrates *persistent* faith. She leaves a comfortable life in Ur and moves to Harran and then to Canaan. At age sixty-five, she begins to live a nomadic tent life. Sarah takes matters into her own hands when she gives Hagar to Abraham to conceive a child. Initially, she laughs when she hears that she will become pregnant in her old age. But then she believes that God will be faithful to his promise to do what is humanly impossible. After living with the stigma of barrenness, Sarah becomes a mother at age ninety and is a strong protector of her son, the long-promised heir.

Sarah hears and believes God's promise that she will be a mother of nations and kings, although she never meets her grandchildren or even her son Isaac's wife Rebekah. Although the Lord promises Abraham the land of Canaan, Sarah doesn't live to see their first official piece of property because the first parcel of land they own is her burial plot—the cave of Machpelah in Hebron—which Abraham buys when she dies at age 127.[14]

Sarah's faith endures through the trials of her family life, through the pain and waiting, and through all the highs and lows of a long life. As a result, she holds the distinguished position of being the matriarch of Israel and the mother of our faith.

Reflect on the Chapter

* Abraham failed to protect Sarah by twice asking her to pretend to be his sister. In what ways did God honor and protect Sarah when her husband did not?
* Abraham exploited Sarah, but Sarah also exploited her slave, Hagar. In what ways did God honor and protect Hagar? And how did Hagar respond to God in faith?
* Despite Abraham's and Sarah's failings and flaws, they also demonstrated persistent faith. Describe any ways they showed trust in God's promises.

Reflect on Your Life

* After ten years of trying for a child, Sarah got tired of waiting and took matters into her own hands. She forced Hagar to sleep with her husband so she could have a child through a surrogate. Describe a time when waiting on God's promises was hard and you may have been tempted to take matters into your own hands.
* Even though Sarah's womb was as good as dead, she had faith that God would bring life from the dead. Describe a

time when you trusted in God's promises even though it may have felt humanly impossible.

* In her darkest hour, Hagar felt seen by God, and that gave her hope and faith to go on. Have you ever felt seen by God? How did that impact your life?

Take Your Bold Step

* Reflect on a time when you put your own needs ahead of those of someone else, perhaps someone who needed your protection. Ask God for forgiveness and guidance on how to repair that wrong, then take that step toward reconciliation.

* Waiting can feel passive, but waiting in faith is a bold step of trust. In which area of your life are you waiting for God's promises to be fulfilled? How can you wait in faith and keep your heart open, tender, and expectant?

Breath Prayer

(Inhale)   *El-roi,*

(Exhale)   you are the God who sees me.

CHAPTER 5

Tamar in the Transformation of Judah

GENESIS 38

Tamar is a controversial figure. Some accuse her of seducing her father-in-law, Judah.[1] Scripture and Jewish tradition, however, praise Tamar. Ancient law codes inform us that she acts within her legal right, which Judah denied her. Ultimately, Tamar plays a pivotal role in the transformation of Judah from scoundrel to godly leader. Judah surprisingly becomes the head of the house of Israel, leading to King David and eventually to the Messiah—all through Perez, Judah's son through Tamar.

How does all this come about?

The final and longest narrative in Genesis is "the Joseph story," which runs from chapters 37 through 50. Embedded in this is the story of the fall and rise of Judah, the fourth son of Leah and Jacob. In Genesis 38, the story of Judah and Tamar disrupts the narrative flow of Joseph's story with an intentionally crafted literary design to shift our attention from Joseph to Judah as the key figure in redemptive history.

Joseph is the firstborn son of Jacob's favorite wife, Rachel. She is the only wife he wanted. Before Jacob married Rachel, his father-in-law, Laban, tricked Jacob into marrying Rachel's older, seemingly less-attractive sister, Leah, who gives birth to multiple sons. Rachel, who struggles with infertility, dies giving birth to her second son, Benjamin.

Joseph is introduced as his father's favorite son, and everyone knows it. Although he's the eleventh of twelve sons, Jacob gives him a coat of honor. The Hebrew word for this special long-sleeved coat, *kutōnet* (Gen 37:23), is most often used for the tunic worn by the priests.[2] Because of Joseph's preferential treatment by his father and his peacocking around his brothers, the reader of Genesis 37 is told three times that they "hated him," "hated him all the more," and then "hated him all the more" (Gen 37:4, 5, 8). Their jealous hatred bursts into a murder plot when opportunity arises. They strip Joseph of his *kuttoneth* and throw him into a pit (Gen 37:23–24).

The ten brothers' first plan is to let him die in the pit to be eaten by animals. But Judah's voice prevails as he suggests they might instead sell him to an approaching band of merchants heading to Egypt, rather than have blood on their hands (Gen 37:26–27). Although Judah prevents Joseph's immediate murder, the brothers profit financially from trafficking their brother. And in their minds, they place his blood on his slave owner. Their future words indicate their assumption that he would die in slavery (Gen 42:32; 44:20).

Examine Please: Do You Recognize the Tunic?

The sons cover up their deed by dipping Joseph's special tunic in the blood of a goat. Then they take the tunic back to their father and say, "We found this. Examine it to see whether it is your son's robe" (Gen 37:32). Their father recognizes it and breaks down weeping, tearing his cloak, wailing that Joseph has been torn apart by a wild animal. He refuses to be comforted, declaring that he will go down to Sheol mourning the death of his son (v. 35). Meanwhile, Joseph is sold to Potiphar, the pharaoh's captain of the guard.

Judah Lives with the Canaanites

In the next scene, Judah has left his family to live with the Canaanites (Gen 38). Abraham and Isaac had specifically commanded their children not to marry Canaanites (Gen 24:3; 28:1). Judah, however, not only marries a Canaanite but also, from all indications, *becomes* a Canaanite. He has successfully assimilated into their community with status and wealth.[3] In Judah's taking a wife, we generally miss the bluntness of Judah's actions by the polite translations of Genesis 38:2–3, such as the NIV: "There Judah met the daughter of a Canaanite man named Shua. He married her and made love to her; she became pregnant and gave birth to a son, who was named Er." Sounds nice and sweet.

A more direct translation lacks the language of marriage or love and reflects a rapid sequence of events: "There Judah saw the daughter of a Canaanite man named Shua, and he took her, and he came into her, and she became pregnant and gave birth to a son, and he named him Er" (my translation). The words "saw" and "took" used in the second verse have a rather dark history in biblical Hebrew. The Hebrew wording that usually alludes to sex within marriage ("to take a wife," *laqah ishah*) is not used in this sentence, although there is no language of violence.[4] However, the sequence of the two verbs "saw" and "took" describes the actions of the woman in Genesis 3:6 after the serpent tempted her to blatantly disobey God and eat from the only forbidden tree: "When the woman saw that the tree was good for food . . . she took of its fruit" (NRSVue). The next sequence using "saw" and "took" describes the actions of the rebellious sons of Elohim in Genesis 6:2: "the sons of God saw that the daughters of humans were good; and they took for themselves women of all that they chose" (my translation).

The sequence is next used in Genesis 12:15. When Abram and Sarai go down to Egypt, Pharaoh's officials saw and took Sarai and brought her into Pharaoh's house to be one of his women. Then, in Genesis 34:2, Dinah, daughter of Jacob, goes to visit the local women in the city. There, Shechem, the prince of the city, is attracted to her. He "saw her . . . took her," "lay" with her, and "debased" her (translation from the Hebrew).[5] Later, David "saw" that Bathsheba was "good" in appearance and commanded his messengers to "take" her and bring her to him, and he "lay" with her (2 Sam 11:2–4, translation from the Hebrew).[6]

Back to Genesis 38. Judah has three sons with his unnamed wife. The first son's name, Er (er), can mean "protected, protector" or "awake, watchful." He is none of these things. But if the two letters of his name in Hebrew are reversed, they spell *evil*, which quickly becomes a better descriptor. Their second son is named Onan (*onan*). A similarly spelled Hebrew word missing the final *n* and different vowels, *awen*, means "disaster, sin, or injustice," which also describe the story of Onan's shortened life. Finally, Shelah is the name of their third son.

The reporting of events continues at a rapid-fire pace, ending in the death of first Er and then Onan:

> Judah took a wife for Er his firstborn; her name was Tamar. But Er, Judah's firstborn, was wicked in the sight of the LORD, and the LORD put him to death. Then Judah said to Onan, "Go in to your brother's wife and perform the duty of a brother-in-law to her; raise up offspring for your brother." But since Onan knew that the offspring would not be his, he spilled his semen on the ground whenever he went in to his brother's wife, so that he would not give offspring to his brother. What he did was displeasing in the sight of the LORD, and he put him to death also" (Gen 38:6–10 NRSVue).

No explanation is given regarding the wickedness done by Er, only Yahweh's opinion by the narrator that "Er, Judah's firstborn, was evil in the eyes of the LORD, and the LORD caused him to die" (Gen 38:7, my translation). Onan's evil, however, is specified.

Onan's Evil: Greed and Sexual Abuse

Onan knows that if he produces an heir for his deceased older brother, this child would receive the larger inheritance of his firstborn brother. If Er has no heir, then Onan gets the larger share.[7] Onan, conversely, does not decline the opportunity to have frequent sex with his sister-in-law. We aren't told whether Tamar is considered Onan's wife, for she continues to be called the wife of his brother (Gen 38:8). But we are informed that Onan repeatedly has sex with Tamar but always withdraws and climaxes on the ground. The Hebrew puts it this way: "And so it was that whenever he came into the wife of his brother, that he ruined [or corrupted] his seed to the ground so that he would not give seed [offspring] to his brother" (Gen 38:9, my translation).

Interestingly, in the book of Genesis, there are only three circumstances where these four Hebrew words occur together: evil (*ra'*), corrupt (or ruin, destroy, *shahat*), death (*mwt*) by God, contrasted with a person who is called righteous (*tsadiq*).[8] These are the narratives of the flood in Genesis 6:5–13; Sodom and Gomorrah in Genesis 19:13–14; and Er and Onan in Genesis 38:9–10. The next time these three words occur together is in reference to the Israelites' pagan worship of a golden calf in Exodus 32:7–10, with the ritual behaviors of sex and sacrifice that go along with it. (Though these acts are not explicitly described in the biblical text, the original audience would have understood what these practices entailed. This understanding comes from archaeological evidence, which reveals the kinds of ritual behaviors—such as sexual acts and sacrifices—commonly associated with ancient cultic worship.) These narratives point to a level of malevolence in which a person or group of people are violating others to such an extent that it warrants capital punishment by God.

Onan abuses Tamar, repeatedly breaking covenant and violating the honor of his brother's wife, whom he was expected to protect. The injustices against Tamar are a mirror of the injustices against Joseph, occurring in a similar time frame.[9] After the death of Onan, Judah assumes that Tamar is the cause of the death of his two sons and fears the death of his third son, Shelah. To be rid of Tamar, Judah sends her back to her father's house.

Tamar's Legal Option

Tamar is trapped within the customs of her time. After Tamar is sent back to her father's house, the household of Judah abandons her. She is neither an independent widow who can marry outside of Judah's family (since she is still technically betrothed to his son Shelah), nor is she a dependent wife, as Judah has postponed the marriage to Shelah indefinitely. With inheritance coming through the sons, her legal rights for protection are violated and provision denied.

What options were available to a woman in her circumstances?

As a widow, if she were to marry outside the family, she would forfeit all possessions and the inheritance of her late husband.[10] Tamar is left without a way to protect the lineage of her late husband or provide for herself.

The custom throughout the ancient Near East to protect widows and the family lineage is called "levirate marriage." In Scripture we see this practice in the book of Ruth, carried out by Boaz. This concept seems peculiar to the Western mind, but ancient societies placed great importance on producing an heir to preserve the family lineage, secure the birthright inheritance of the land, and ensure the widow's well-being. Mariottini describes the levirate law as "designed to protect a widow's inheritance rights within her father-in-law's family."[11] Marten Stol describes levirate marriage this way:

> If after the death of her husband a widow marries her husband's brother it is called a levirate marriage. . . . It is the interests of the family as a whole, not of individuals, which were considered paramount. The "bride" (kallatu) does not just belong to the bridegroom but she is the bride of the head of the family or of the whole family. . . . The Hittites, the Hurrians (in Nuzi), the Assyrians, the Canaanites and the Israelites all practised levirate marriage . . . [which] seems to be restricted to the period between 1500 and 1000 BC.[12]

In Israel, the levirate marriage was with a brother-in-law or a close relative. But in several other nations of the ancient Near East, the "Levirate marriage was the obligation of a brother, father, or nearest kin to provide a male heir for a deceased man through his wife. . . . That the levirate duty could pass from brother to father was not unusual."[13]

Since Judah withholds his son Shelah as the kinsman redeemer for Tamar, Judah himself is the next in line to fulfill the responsibilities and obligations of the law.

After a Long Time . . .

Years pass. Tamar has been waiting in limbo for many, many years. Judah's wife dies. After the customary time of mourning, Judah travels to Timnah for the shearing of the sheep with his friend Hirah the Adullamite. When Tamar is told of Judah's plans, she takes the opportunity to seek justice: "She put off her widow's garments, put on a veil, wrapped herself up, and sat down at the entrance to Enaim, which is on the road to Timnah. She saw that Shelah was grown up, yet she had not been given to him in marriage. When Judah saw her, he thought her to be a prostitute, for she had covered her face" (Gen 38:14–15 NRSVue).

Tamar seems to know Judah's character well enough to be sure that if she merely puts on a veil and presents herself as sexually available at the side of the road that Judah will make an offer to have sex with her. Yes, he would be honorable enough to pay a woman for her "services," but that's it. Tamar sits down by the road in a place called *pethah enayim*, the gate of Enayim, which could be translated "Open Eyes." Judah does not recognize Tamar, but her eyes are open to see that Judah has abandoned his legal and moral responsibility for her.[14]

They discuss payment, and he agrees to give her a pledge of his signet, cord, and staff (Gen 38:17–18). Archaeological analysis informs us that these items bore specific significance in the ancient world: "They appear to be the three most prominent signs of identification in antiquity, at least among high-ranking personalities like Judah."[15] The signet ring, cord, and staff indicate that Judah is a man of significant means in the Canaanite community, and "the marked staff may have identified Judah as the head of his clan."[16] Therefore, when he sends the kid goat as promised payment but Tamar can't be found, Judah wants to save face and sends the messenger back home.

However, Tamar is not looking for payment but for a tangible guarantee that Judah will fulfill his responsibility to do right by her. Unbeknownst to Judah, Tamar is seeking the fulfillment of Judah's oath as father-in-law to redeem her, not just his promise to pay her a goat. In her actions, she hints at the future—when she will receive a guarantee that her son will be the one chosen to continue the Judean dynasty.[17] This is her last-ditch effort in her pursuit of justice.

Examine Please: Do You Recognize These?

About three months later, Judah finds out that Tamar is pregnant. His immediate response is, "Bring her out, and let her be burned" (Gen 38:24). Although Judah is a man of means, Carol Meyers shows that Judah did not have the authority to condemn Tamar to death by burning or by any other means.[18] No doubt he is trying to ruin her reputation, hoping to finally be rid of her once and for all! As Judah showed earlier, his concern is for his own reputation, to save face (Gen 38:23).

Tamar, however, responds with boldness in the face of his threat. "As she was being brought out, she sent a message to her father-in-law: 'I am pregnant by the man who owns these,' she said. And she added, 'Examine, please, whose seal and cord and staff these are'" (Gen 38:25, my translation).

Here we make the important connection between Genesis 37 and 38. In the Hebrew, Tamar uses the same words that Judah and his brothers spoke to their father Jacob when handing him Joseph's bloody tunic: "Examine please (*hakker-na*)" or "Do you recognize" the tunic? Judah is now confronted with these words: "Examine please (*hakker-na*)" or "Do you recognize these?" (Gen 37:32–33). Just as Jacob "recognized" the tunic as Joseph's, here Judah "recognizes" the signet ring, cord, and staff as his own (Gen 37:32–33; 38:25–26). The very words that recall the wrongs Judah instigated against Joseph and his father sound in his own ears and slap him out of two decades of complacency and denial.

When Judah acknowledges that the items belong to him, he yields, declaring, "'She is more righteous than I, since I wouldn't give her to my son Shelah.' And he did not sleep with her again" (Gen 38:26). The statement that Judah did not lie with Tamar again "presupposes that sex with his daughter-in-law was legitimate as a means of fulfilling a family obligation, even if it was irregular, and it should have been Shelah who took this action."[19]

Although Tamar's actions were a daring way to obtain what was right, Scripture maintains her integrity in subverting the power structure and overturning the injustice done to her and her future progeny.

Tamar's Righteousness

What is meant by Judah's statement that Tamar is "more righteous than I"? In Israel and the ancient Near East, "righteousness" (*tsadeqah*) was a relationship word signifying "that things are right between two parties."[20] Righteousness implies faithfulness, along with respectful and considerate behavior toward another, even and especially in the face of adversity and responsibility. Everyone is held accountable for their actions, and order is maintained through strong community relationships.[21]

King Saul speaks to David using nearly the identical words as Judah spoke to Tamar. When Saul learns that David refused to take his life when he had the ideal opportunity, he declares to David, "You are more righteous than I" (1 Sam 24:17). The implication is that David had treated their relationship "more seriously and given more heed to it" than Saul had.[22] "Unlike the modern focus on the individual, the ANE focus was on the community. Correct behaviour was that which recognized our mutual dependency and showed 'kindness, faithfulness, and, as circumstances arose, helpful compassion to the poor or the suffering.'"[23] Where there was an imbalance of power between two parties, the expectation was that the weaker party could trust that the stronger party would do what was right on behalf of the weaker party.[24]

In Tamar's case, she couldn't trust the stronger party to act on her behalf. But her bold actions provide Judah the opportunity to open his eyes to see his wrongs and confess that she was more righteous than he was. Old Testament scholar Belinda Tan concludes, "Tamar is portrayed as righteous because she is faithful to her role as a daughter-in-law in Judah's household. Conversely, Judah is not righteous, because he is unfaithful to his duties as her father-in-law and the paterfamilias. Yet, by admitting that Tamar has done rightly, but he has not, Judah is redeemed."[25]

Thus, Tamar becomes the only woman to receive the designation of "righteous" in the Old Testament. Judah clearly failed in his responsibility toward Tamar. She, however, found a way to honor her late husband and protect their family lineage, which Judah recognizes as righteousness (ṣedāqâ), doing that which is right and just.

The Rest of the Story

Tamar gives birth to twin boys, Perez and Zerah. Sometime after Tamar's confrontation of Judah, he takes Tamar and their sons back to Jacob and his brothers. While Scripture does not record the narrative of their return, that they did return perhaps represents Judah's return to his faith and his roots. After rejoining Jacob's household, Judah travels to Egypt with his brothers to buy grain during the famine. There, he unknowingly meets his brother Joseph, who they know at this point only as the second most powerful figure in Egypt after Pharaoh.

Joseph tests his brothers, creating a scenario that requires them to come back to Egypt with their youngest brother Benjamin, Joseph's only full-blooded brother. When Joseph threatens to keep Benjamin as his slave, Judah's reply to this formidable leader in Egypt demonstrates his change in character. In a lengthy plea, Judah requests that Joseph "please let your servant remain here as my lord's slave in place of the boy, and let the boy return with his brothers. How can I go back to my father if the boy is not with me? No! Do not let me see the misery that would come on my father" (Gen 44:33–34).

Judah's transformation reveals he is no longer jealous of his father's favorites. Now instead of trying to save his reputation or do what only benefits him, he asserts his leadership by being willing to lay down his life in exchange for his younger, favored brother, Benjamin. This becomes the moment that Joseph reveals his identity to Judah and his brothers. Without Judah's drastic change brought on by Tamar's bold confrontation, this encounter with Joseph could have looked very different.

Legacy of Tamar

Tamar's actions initiate a powerful redemption story in the Old Testament. Her story is strategically placed near the beginning of the Joseph story, moving salvation history forward and reminding us that God's calling has always been to draw all people from all nations into his grand story. God delights in working through bold but overlooked and underestimated women to bring forth his purposes.

If Tamar had not taken the risk to accomplish what was right, Judah would not have been held accountable for his moral failures. Her courage turns the tide of her life and of Judah's life, family, and lineage, which were all in jeopardy.

In studying Tamar's story, we can see its importance in the overarching story of the Bible. The birth of Tamar's twins, Perez and Zerah, mirrors the birth of Jacob and Esau to Rebecca, in which the younger wrestles to be born first. This theme of reversal, the unexpected, such as in this story where the younger takes precedence over the elder, is a recurring motif in biblical narratives, symbolizing divine intervention and the overturning of societal norms. And the scarlet cord tied around Zerah's wrist foreshadows the story of Rahab, who uses a scarlet cord to mark her window to let the marching Israelites know to save her and her family from destruction. Rahab, like Tamar, becomes part of the Messianic lineage, further emphasizing God's redemptive work through unexpected individuals (Gen 38:28 and Josh 2:18, 21; Matt 1:5).

As with Jacob and Esau, Tamar's second twin, Perez, takes the lead over Zerah, continuing the line that leads to King David and, eventually, to Jesus Christ (Gen 38:27–30; Ruth 4:12; 1 Chr 2:4–15). Tamar's legacy is celebrated in Bethlehem when the women praise her as an exemplar of faithfulness and perseverance after Ruth gives birth to Obed, the grandfather of David (Ruth 4:12). This connection underscores Tamar's pivotal role in the lineage of Israel's great king.

David himself honors Tamar's name by naming one of his daughters Tamar, the sister of Absalom (2 Sam 13; 1 Chr 3:9). Absalom too names his daughter Tamar (2 Sam 14:27). A city in Judah is also named Tamar, signifying her enduring influence in the region's history (1 Kgs 9:18; Ezek 47:19; 48:28). And finally, Tamar takes her place as one of the few women explicitly listed in the genealogy of Jesus Christ (Matt 1:3–5; Luke 3:33).

Tamar was abused and mistreated by a powerful family with no one to advocate for her, not her father-in-law or even her own father. But she doesn't allow her circumstances to beat her down. She waits for the right time to act boldly to honor her late husband and preserve his line. She doesn't act impulsively, but she executes a well-thought-through plan for recourse. Her story is a reminder to us that while we may feel forgotten, God hasn't forgotten the Tamars who are neglected or abused. We may not feel like we have an earthly advocate. But God is our advocate. And God weaves Tamar into the line of David and Jesus. None of our stories are void of hope.

Reflect on the Chapter

* Although her actions were unconventional and are considered controversial outside of ancient law, Tamar is the only

woman to receive the designation of "righteous" in the Old Testament. In what ways was Tamar more righteous than Judah?

* If Tamar had not held Judah accountable, he may not have turned his life around. Describe Judah's transformation in Scripture.
* In what ways is Tamar honored in Scripture? And what is her role in the larger redemptive story?

Reflect on Your Life

* Describe an experience when you benefited from someone keeping you accountable for your actions.
* Describe a time when you spoke up and acted to keep someone accountable for their actions.
* Have you ever been misjudged, forgotten, or even abused and neglected like Tamar? If so, how does Tamar's story give you hope?

Take Your Bold Step

* God cares for the vulnerable, especially the widow and the fatherless (Jas 1:27: Isa 1:17; Deut 10:18). What specific way can you look out for the vulnerable in your community?
* Is there someone in your life whom you have misjudged or mistreated? How can you confess and make things right with that person?

Breath Prayer

(Inhale)   Jesus, my Shepherd,
(Exhale)   lead me in paths of righteousness.

CHAPTER 6

Women Who Instigate the Exodus

EXODUS 1–2

The beauty of looking at the strategic role of women at key junctures in Scripture is realizing that none of them expected to be honored or make history. Women in the opening chapters of Exodus risk their lives to disobey the highest human authority. No earthly reward is in sight for them. No gain of status is expected. They aren't trying to be heroes. They endanger their lives by doing what is right and upholding the value of life. When faced with opposition, they don't lose hope but courageously do what they can to give life, save lives, and protect lives.

Creation Blessing Continues, but So Does the Grief of Brokenness

Genesis closes with the Israelites living peacefully in Egypt during Joseph's rule as second in command. The story of the exodus begins with their wildly successful population growth, repeating the creation blessing from Genesis 1:28 to be fruitful, multiply, and fill the land (Exod 1:6–7). A portion of God's promise to Abraham and Sarah toward becoming a large nation is being fulfilled.

The story swiftly moves from covenant blessing to an echo from Genesis 3:16 of the grief and mental anguish from family circumstances that Eve, Sarah, Rebekah, Leah, Rachel, and Tamar experienced. Hardships pass down from their families to the nation of their descendants, the Israelites.

A new pharaoh rises to power who has forgotten Joseph's history. Instead, he is afraid that the rapidly increasing number of Israelites will revolt against him. His first tactic for tamping down their expansion is to subject them to harsh slavery.[1] However, his success in reducing their growth fails, largely because he sees only the males as a threat to his kingdom.

The Women's First Transgressive Act Against Egypt Gives Life

Hebrew women first set the stage for the exodus by giving birth to healthy babies and raising them to adulthood.[2] This may sound like an insignificant or insulting role to Westernized women today. But in the ancient Near East during this time, the mortality rate averaged about fifty percent for the first five years of life.[3] Egyptian lifespan estimates were thirty-three years for men and twenty-nine years for women.[4] Women with multiple births lived even shorter lives.

As marginalized people, the Israelites' mortality rates should have been even higher and their life spans shorter than those of the Egyptians. But amazingly, "the more they were oppressed, the more they multiplied and spread; so the Egyptians came to dread the Israelites and worked them ruthlessly" (Exod 1:12–13). The fortitude of the Israelite women to endure the natural hazards of childbirth during their "bitter" and "harsh" (v. 14) slavery is a marvel. The women are "waging a kind of war" against the pharaoh through their fruitfulness.[5] The fact that the Hebrew women keep giving birth in such difficult times is a sign of hope and defiance.

The more Pharaoh beats them down, the more their population grows. In frustration, he commands the midwives to kill every male baby born to a Hebrew woman (Exod 1:10–16). While Pharaoh "discounts the women's power and character, . . . most importantly for us readers and people of faith, Scripture does not."[6] Pharaoh's plan is foiled by those he disregards: the women.

The Women's Second Transgressive Act Against Egypt Saves Lives

Only Jacob, his twelve sons, and two women, Shiphrah and Puah, are named in the opening chapter of the book of Exodus. The men are named for genealogical purposes. We aren't given the genealogy of Shiphrah and Puah. Their names are included because of their bravery.

Scholars aren't certain if Shiphrah and Puah were Egyptian or Israelite because the Hebrew can be interpreted as either "midwives of the Hebrews" or "Hebrew midwives." Not even the etymology of their names solidifies a clue. Shiphrah and Puah are the first people identified as resisting the king of Egypt by cleverly refusing to comply with his murderous command to kill every male child born to a Hebrew. Whether Egyptian or Hebrew, they are collaborators with God and women. They are given a place of honor in this central story of the Israelite people: the exodus from slavery.

When summoned by Pharaoh, Shiphrah and Puah know they have been caught defying his edict. Pharaoh is the most powerful man in Egypt, yet Shiphrah and Puah choose to do what is right in the eyes of God because they know they answer to a higher authority than Pharaoh. Their fear of God is the source of their boldness (Exod 1:17).

They demonstrate courageous advocacy to save lives. When Pharaoh confronts them, they cleverly rely on Pharaoh's sense of ethnic superiority and his ignorance of women and the birthing process. Shiphrah and Puah claim that the Hebrew women are more vigorous than the Egyptian women, playing to his view of the Israelite slaves as "less than human" by using a word that could imply they are more like "animals" (*ḥāywōt*) in the way they give birth quickly before a midwife can arrive (Exod 1:19).[7] They use his prejudice to their advantage, which works against his evil purposes.

In this first chapter, God honors these midwives who fear him. While the pharaoh is unnamed, Shiphrah and Puah are named, blessed by God, and given families and homes of their own (Exod 1:20–21).

The Women's Third Transgressive Act Against Egypt Protects Lives

When Pharaoh's attempt to kill baby boys through the midwives is foiled, he gives a command directly to the people: "Every Hebrew boy that is born you must throw into the Nile, but let every girl live" (Exod 1:22). Pharaoh thinks that girls and women are no threat to his empire.

Pharaoh's belief in his male supremacy is so sufficiently blinding that he misses the fact that the females he overlooks are the very ones who initiate the rescue of the Israelite people from slavery through peaceful subversion: doing what is right. There are no strikes nor outcries from the women. They collaborate to save and protect lives. The women act boldly and faithfully, refusing to comply with evil edicts, and God uses them to begin the rescue plan.

In Exodus 2, an Israelite slave woman, a Levite, gives birth to a baby boy and spares his life, hiding him for three months. When she can no longer hide him, she creatively obeys the king's command to throw newborn boys into the Nile. This mother makes a tiny papyrus ark coated with tar and pitch, lays her baby in it, wrapped in a Hebrew blanket, and places him in the Nile. It's no coincidence that the Hebrew word used for Moses's basket is the same as that used for Noah's ark, *tevah*.[8]

The baby's big sister follows the little ark from a distance "to see what would happen to him" as it makes its way along the reeds of the Nile (Exod 2:4). She was between the ages of six and twelve years old.[9]

Pause a minute to notice that the mother, daughter, and baby are not yet named in the story. From the outside, they are insignificant slaves of no status, nameless to the powers and people of the prevailing empire. In later chapters we're given their names: Jochebed, Miriam, and Moses.

The little ark stops among the reeds along the riverbank where Pharaoh's daughter comes to bathe with her personal slaves in attendance. This woman of wealth and influence sees the curious ark and asks one of her slaves to bring it to her. As a woman of privilege, she can easily turn a blind eye to the troubles of the vulnerable around her. But she chooses to draw close to see the baby and hear him crying. She opens her eyes and her heart and has compassion for him, saying, "This is one of the Hebrew babies" (Exod 2:6).

With this opportunity in sight, the baby's big sister moves into action. God has put her in the right place at the right time. She immediately recognizes and seizes the moment with boldness and cleverness.

The young slave girl speaks to the princess, offering to find a Hebrew woman to nurse the baby "for you." "For you" presumes Pharaoh's daughter's intentions, identifying the baby as now belonging to her. These words are prophetic and powerful. Later, Miriam is identified as a prophet (Exod 15:20–21).

Remarkably, she is suggesting that the princess defy her father's command! This could put the slave girl's own life in jeopardy, as she doesn't know how Pharaoh's daughter will respond. Fortunately, seemingly on impulse, Pharaoh's daughter agrees with the slave girl's plan and simply says, "Go." The princess's response mirrors God's later command to Moses from the burning bush: to "go" and deliver his people (Exod 2:8; 3:16).

The brief interaction between the girl and the princess provides continuity between the baby and his Hebrew slave family. The little girl brings her mother—the baby's mother—to Pharaoh's daughter, who pays the mother to nurse her baby boy. By having compassion on a little slave baby, Pharaoh's daughter uses her power to protect and provide for him and his family. In defying her cruel father, she also places herself at risk.

When the baby boy is weaned, his mother returns him to Pharaoh's daughter, who takes him as her son. Back then, a mother typically nursed her child for about three years. In that time, the baby grows from a cute baby to a walking, talking young boy! The princess could have easily changed her mind or had one of her handmaids raise Moses. But she courageously follows through with her decision to adopt the boy and names him Moses, saying, "I drew him out of the water" (Exod 2:10). This in itself is a courageous statement of defiance against Pharaoh's command to drown the baby boys in the Nile, for she instead "drew him out." The princess commits to raising Moses as her own, giving him the privileges of an Egyptian prince.

As Jacqueline Lapsley observes, "Pharaoh's schemes fail because he underestimates the tenacity and creative power of the Hebrew women. In a larger theological sense, Pharaoh fatally underestimates the power of God to work deliverance through the vulnerable—and seemingly powerless—on behalf of the vulnerable."[10]

The bold and sacrificial actions of overlooked women spare the life of an insignificant slave baby. They have no idea that this defenseless boy they risk their lives to protect will become God's vessel to bring down the prevailing powers of Egypt and lead the fledgling nation of Israelites to freedom and the land promised to Abraham, Isaac, and Jacob.

Legacy of the Women in Exodus

The women's life-giving and life-saving insurrection precipitates the overthrow of Pharaoh's murderous power. Carmen Imes calls these women "freedom fighters."[11] Their seemingly small acts of resistance establish a theme of defiance and deliverance, which is foundational to the exodus.

We continue the legacy of these "freedom fighters" whenever we give and protect life. Like Shiphrah and Puah, we may be "midwife-ing" a new thing, which requires a deep faith and fear of God. Like Jochebed, we may be giving birth and nurturing life in ways that are countercultural. Like Miriam, we may speak words or lead in ways that set into motion or help carry out God's plan. Or, like Pharaoh's daughter, we may be called to cross social and ethnic boundaries or commit to loving and raising up the next generation of leaders.

Miriam continues to defy stereotypes as she grows older. After the Israelites cross the Sea of Reeds, miraculously delivered from the Egyptian military forces, Miriam leads the women in dance and song, where she is called a prophet (Exod 15:20–21). This passage represents one of the earliest Hebrew songs in the Bible.[12] According to the testimony of Scripture, she is an unmarried female prophet and leader of God's people. The prophet Micah recalls Miriam's leadership alongside that of her brothers, saying, "Indeed, I brought you up from the land of Egypt and ransomed you from the house of slavery, and I sent before you Moses, Aaron, and Miriam" (Mic 6:4 NASB1995). Her name remains a popular Jewish name for centuries, as attested in the New Testament, which translates Miriam from Greek into English as Mary.

Miriam and the women of the exodus embody God's values, "values that point toward the liberation of all humanity, no matter what the boundaries defining human identity may be, in defiance of all socially and politically and culturally constructed limitations."[13]

Bold women and their godly actions continue to move the biblical narrative forward. Shiphrah and Puah, Jochebed and Miriam, and Pharaoh's daughter simply open their hearts to love and do what they can in their role to help the one in front of them. We, too, may have no idea of what God is doing through us when we take risks to stand against wrongs and injustice, but God sees, and our words and deeds are recorded in eternity.

> He has told you, O mortal, what is good,
> and what does the LORD require of you
> but to do justice and to love kindness
> and to walk humbly with your God?
> (Micah 6:8 NRSVue)

Reflect on the Chapter

- How does the book of Genesis conclude, and how does the book of Exodus open?
- Describe the women's three transgressive acts against Egypt that Dr. Faro names in each section.
- What do you think gave each of these women the boldness to act or speak on behalf of this slave baby?

Reflect on Your Life

- God indiscriminately used women of different ethnicities, ages, and socioeconomic backgrounds in this chapter. Which woman in this chapter do you identify with most, and why? How do you see yourself carrying out the legacy of one or more of these women?

* Miriam followed and waited to see what would happen to her brother and then found herself at the right place and at the right time. Describe a time when God gave you an opportunity that you couldn't have orchestrated yourself. How did you respond?

* At the time, these women did not know that God would use their selfless, bold actions to weave a redemptive story, culminating in the rescue of their people through Moses. Think of a situation where a person was faithful to do what was right and God used it for a greater purpose.

Take Your Bold Step

* It would have been easy for these women to feel like their actions would not make a difference in light of Pharaoh's edict; yet they just did what they could for the one in front of them. What situation in your life feels overwhelming to you? What is one action step you can take in your role?

* Pharaoh's daughter steps out of her comfort zone to see and hear the cries of the slave baby. She allows her heart to feel compassion, which then informs her bold actions. Think of a person you might be holding at a distance. Ask God to give you a heart of compassion to see that person as he sees them. How can you use your influence or privilege in that situation?

Breath Prayer

(Inhale)   God of Rescue,
(Exhale)   give me courage to do the next right thing.

CHAPTER 7

Rahab's Faith Prepares the Way into the Promised Land

JOSHUA 2–6

Scripture is full of reversals of expectations.[1] The story of Rahab is among those at the top of the list. She appears in the beginning of the book of Joshua when the Israelites are poised to enter the promised land. Controversies about her occupation and her character abound. But the Scripture commends her faith and her courage as she assists the Israelites in a pivotal moment in their history.

In Deuteronomy, Moses commands the Israelites to destroy the inhabitants of Canaan, to "make no treaty with them, and show them no mercy. Do not intermarry with them" lest they lead the Israelites to abandon worshiping Yahweh and instead follow the gods of the Canaanites (Deut 7:2–4).

But then come some surprises in Joshua. The book is often called a "conquest narrative," as the Israelites defeat Canaanite cities to occupy the promised land. But some twists along the way alter our understanding of Deuteronomy's harsh commands. For example, God rewards the faith of Rahab the Canaanite and Caleb and Othniel the Kenizzites (a tribe of the Edomites who were enemies of Israel), while punishing Achan, the unfaithful Israelite.

Set Up for a Surprise

The book of Joshua opens with the death of Moses, with Joshua appointed as his successor to bring God's people into the promised land. Some people mistakenly read God's command in chapter 1 of Joshua to "be strong and courageous" as a call to be brave in battle. The context points instead to being a call to have the fortitude to follow Yahweh faithfully and not to turn aside to worship the foreign gods of the Canaanites (Josh 1:6, 7, 9, 18).

In chapter 2, Rahab demonstrates strength and courage in her loyalty to Yahweh. "In this sense, Rahab corresponds to Joshua as the faithful one of her people who is chosen to lead them to salvation, or, at least to offer it to those who are interested."[2] Several things stand out in the first verse of Joshua 2, which reads, "Then Joshua son of Nun sent from Shittim two men to secretly spy, saying to the spies, 'Go, look over the land, especially Jericho.' So they went and entered the house of a woman, a prostitute named Rahab, and they laid down there" (my translation).

First, this language is reminiscent of two stories in the book of Numbers. Joshua sent two spies to see the land, just as Moses did when he sent twelve spies to see the land in Numbers 13:17–18. This "echo signals to the reader that Joshua's commission is a second attempt to explore the Land, after the failure of the first venture."[3] Earlier in Moses's scouting party, only two of the ten were faithful to Yahweh: Joshua and Caleb. And they were the only men over the age of forty granted access to enter the promised land (Num 13–14).[4] Curiously, while Numbers provides the names and details of the twelve spies Moses sent, the names of the two spies Joshua sent are concealed, while Rahab is named.

Second, in preparation to enter Canaan, the Israelites are encamped across the Jordan River at a place called Shittim ("Acacia Groves"). The mention of a geographic location is rarely a coincidence in the Bible.[5] Only one other significant event in

Shittim is mentioned in the Bible: the last scandal in the wilderness,[6] when the Israelite men begin to indulge in sexual immorality with Moabite women and then bow down to their gods (Num 25:1–2).*

These two negative memories—the failed spy expedition and the Israelites' idolatrous sexual exploits with foreign women—might cause the reader to squirm a little here, wondering where the story is going!

Third, the words used in the last part of Joshua 2:1 could imply sexually immoral behavior.[7] The two spies Joshua sent from Shittim "went and entered the house of a woman, a prostitute, and her name was Rahab, and they laid down there (Josh 2:1, my translation). Although the verbs "went" in and "laid down," ("literally, 'came' and 'lay there'— are often used elsewhere of sexual intercourse; see, e.g. Gen 6:4; 16:2; 30:2; 34:7; 39:7, 10), the text here carefully avoids the suggestion that the spies and Rahab had any sexual relations."[8] But the reader is left hanging.

With these hints of intrigue and shady behavior from the spies, we follow the narrative with curiosity, anticipating a turn of affairs, so to speak. But instead of an expected twist, we get a shocker that reframes the way God wants his people to think about the conquest and reshapes the way he wants *us* to read Joshua.

Rahab's Vocation

The introduction to Rahab's vocation in Joshua 2:1 is described in Hebrew by the word *zonah*. Throughout Scripture, the word *zonah* refers to a prostitute, or "fornicator." The same word is also used metaphorically for idolators, people who are unfaithful to Yahweh through alliances with foreign gods.

---

* The prophet Micah likewise recalls this black mark in Israel's history, "My people, remember what Balak king of Moab plotted and what Balaam son of Beor answered. Remember your journey from Shittim to Gilgal, that you may know the righteous acts of the LORD" (Mic 6:5).

Historical records show that in ancient times, prostitutes could be financially stable innkeepers who doubled as tavern owners. It wasn't uncommon for their business to be located by the walled parts of a city,[9] which could be considered "the disreputable outskirts . . . in the outlying quarters away from the daily life of the respectable inhabitants of the town."[10] The profession of prostitution has never been highly regarded.[11]

To raise Rahab's status, Jewish tradition and Josephus try to soften her reputation by calling her an innkeeper, for they hold Rahab in high esteem. [12] However, as Michael Fishbane points out, "There is no reason to doubt the original ascription of harlotry. It provides an ironic element in the narrative of salvation."[13]

In sum, Rahab is likely a prostitute who is a woman of substance with her own establishment, an unmarried protector of her extended family. And her bold faith reframes the expectations of Israel as they prepare to enter the promised land.[14]

The Not-So-Stealthy Spies and Rahab's Lie

The two spies are clearly not good at their assigned task.[15] The king of Jericho immediately learns of their presence and whereabouts. His messengers come to Rahab's inn demanding that she turn them over. Instead, she risks her life to hide them and lies to protect them, sending the king's messengers off into the hills to search for them (Josh 2:2–5).

Treason against the king demands her death.[16] But Rahab's life is on the line regardless of her decision. She knows that the Israelites wiped out the armies of Egypt; King Og of Bashan; and Sihon, king of the Amorites (Num 21:33–35; Deut 3:1–11). Given this history, she has no reason to expect mercy from the Israelites. Yet Rahab chooses her allegiance. It's neither to the spies nor to the king of Jericho. Her loyalty is soon declared to Yahweh.

Although the Bible attributes no wrongdoing to Rahab in this story, many scholars harshly criticize her not only for her vocation in Jericho but also for being a liar.

Scripture *does* condemn lying about a person to smear their reputation (Exod 20:16). Scripture also condemns lying to gain someone's favor or to bring personal gain (Lev 19:15–16; Prov 6:16–19). And Scripture condemns lying to cover one's own sin or wrongdoing (Prov 28:13). However, Scripture does not condemn lying to a wicked, unjust ruler seeking to murder innocent people or those on a mission from God. For example, Shiphrah and Puah, the midwives of the exodus story, risk their lives by lying to Pharaoh to save the lives of the Hebrew slave babies. God rewards them for their courage. "Just as women were instrumental in the exodus of Israel from Egypt, so a woman is significant in Israel's entrance into the promised land."[17] God looks at the heart and judges the motives. Whereas I don't recommend lying and would hope to find a better solution, let God judge the one as innocent who lies to someone in power to protect or save lives.

Nevertheless, some scholars have described Rahab as a lying "trickster."[18] One finds her story "dark and disturbing," calling Rahab a dominating and aggressive woman, a prostitute by whom the spies have "been mastered and ensnared by their Canaanite counterpart."[19] Others reproach the spies for falling prey to her snare and breaking the strict Mosaic law that demanded her and her family's death along with the rest of Jericho. Another finds the spies and Joshua "in direct disobedience to the Mosaic rules for holy war in Deuteronomy."[20]

These condemnations entirely miss how Joshua's narrative framework fits into Scripture's redemptive storyline. Contrary to these denunciations, "the story of Rahab confirms God's welcome to all people, whatever their condition."[21] As Andrzej Toczyski states,

She was the foreigner who, in advance, was supposed to be condemned to death because of Israelite laws. She was the woman who was supposed to be disregarded because of their male-dominated customs. She was also the prostitute who was supposed to be despised and exploited because of their dismissive attitude to such a profession. Yet, Rahab is the foreign woman and prostitute whose powerful story neutralized and turned upside-down at least some of the pejorative presumptions about her, and impelled the spies to protect her with the obliging oath. It can be argued that, from a broad perspective, the story which Rahab recounted engaged the spies and those whom they represented, to the point of reconsidering their seemingly unchanging laws; thus imagining, at least in some cases, a different scenario of contact other than that accomplished only by "fire and sword."[22]

Rahab's surprising words and actions establish the reversal of expectations for the rest of the book of Joshua and she herself becomes rooted into God's mission from the beginning. She becomes one of those who "call on the name of Yahweh" and is saved (Gen 4:26 LEB).

Rahab's Declaration of Faith

After risking her life to save the spies, Rahab discloses that the whole land knows and fears God's miraculous actions on behalf of the Israelites. Furthermore, she boldly declares her belief in Yahweh as the God above all gods, not only of Israel but of heaven and earth. Here are Rahab's words to the spies as she hides them on her rooftop:

> I know that the LORD has given you this land and that a great fear of you has fallen on us, so that all who live in this country are melting in fear because of you. We have heard how the LORD dried up the water of the Red Sea for you when you

came out of Egypt, and what you did to Sihon and Og, the two kings of the Amorites east of the Jordan, whom you completely destroyed. When we heard of it, our hearts melted in fear and everyone's courage failed because of you, for the LORD your God is God in heaven above and on the earth below. (Josh 2:9–11)

Rahab's statement reveals her expansive understanding of who Yahweh is, what he has done, and what he will accomplish. Specifically, she affirms the following:

1. Canaan would be given to the Israelites (2:9).
2. Everyone in Canaan knew this, therefore "our hearts melted in fear and everyone's courage failed because of you" (2:9, 11).
3. Yahweh worked great marvels for his people in Egypt and in the wilderness (2:10)
4. Yahweh, the God of the Israelites, is the one and only true God: "The LORD your God is God in heaven above and on the earth below" (2:11). In other words, the gods of the Canaanites and other nations are not true gods.

Rahab provides the spies with the information they need for the report they bring back to Joshua. Rahab's declaration provides affirmation of Yahweh's impending victory, so the spies don't spy out any more of Jericho or the rest of the land.

When she helps them escape through a window, she instructs them to hide in the hills for three days and then return to the Israelite camp, which they do (Josh 2:15–16). Their report to Joshua is entirely the words of Rahab (2:24). By her words and actions, Rahab demonstrates strength and courage in her loyalty to Yahweh. The bold faith of this Canaanite woman not only protects the spies but also emboldens them to fulfill their mission.

Rahab Saves Her Family

Rahab's declaration of faith, protection of the spies, and agreement to help them escape is followed by the request that they save her entire family: father, mother, brothers, sisters, and an unspecified "all who belong to them" (Josh 2:13). She is willing to risk her life and the lives of her family based on her faith in Yahweh. Rahab's confession of faith and request of the spies is one of the longest dialogues by a woman in Scripture.[23]

The stipulation for her and her family's rescue is that they all have to be under the protection of her home when Jericho is destroyed. Further, she must hang a red cord from her window so that the Israelites can identify her home.

This scene bears a distant recollection of the night of Passover in Egypt. Each family, including any extended family or friends, had to be in their home with the red blood of the lamb applied to the top and side frames of the door. Only then would the death angel safely pass them by. Rahab's family members believe her and are in her home when the Israelites march around the city wall. Rahab trusts Yahweh to protect them. And death passes over.

Joshua and the spies make good on their oath: "Joshua spared Rahab the prostitute, with her family and all who belonged to her, because she hid the men Joshua had sent as spies to Jericho—and she lives among the Israelites to this day" (Josh 6:25). The echo of the saving of her household is heard in Joshua's final words at the end of the book, when he says, "As for me and my household, we will serve the LORD" (Josh 24:15).

Reversal of Expectations

Rahab's story of faith in action is at the forefront of Israel's entry into the promised land. Through her story, we learn that the promised land is not only for the Israelites but for all who call on the name of Yahweh, the only true God. The expectation to "show them no mercy" (Deut 7:2) is disrupted. The book of Joshua highlights that a Canaanite woman, "against all expectations, seems to show a greater awareness of Israel's faith than the scouts," upending the previous story in Shittim of idolatrous women leading Israelite men astray (Num 25:1–5).[24]

The encounter with Rahab disrupts the harsh expectations of the Law, opening up the realization that God will have mercy on any Canaanite who turns from their gods to follow him. The theme of salvation history running throughout Scripture confirms that what matters to God is not ethnicity but "faith, demonstrated through commitment to Yahweh."[25]

Faith as the basis of right standing with God, and not ethnicity or nationalistic loyalty, continues to be demonstrated in Joshua. This understanding is clarified when Joshua is walking by himself on the eve before the first march around the walls of Jericho:

> He looked up and saw a man standing in front of him with a drawn sword in his hand. Joshua went up to him and asked, "Are you for us or for our enemies?"
>
> "Neither," he replied, "but as commander of the army of the LORD I have now come." Then Joshua fell facedown to the ground in reverence, and asked him, "What message does my Lord have for his servant?"
>
> The commander of the LORD's army replied, "Take off your sandals, for the place where you are standing is holy." And Joshua did so. (Josh 5:13–15)

Joshua recognizes this as a divine encounter, like Moses and the burning bush (Exod 3:1–5) and like Jacob's wrestling match with the divine figure (Gen 32: 24–30).[26] The words of the heavenly being make clear that he is not taking sides with Israel or with their enemies. No, "Neither!" Rather, the commander of the armies of Yahweh wants to know who is on *his* side!

Rahab's story bookends the story of Israel entering the promised land with a surprise element in this first conquest narrative: A native Canaanite is a Yahweh worshiper whose family becomes integrated into the people of God (Joshua 2:1–24 to 6:22–24). The theme of "who is on God's side" is further confirmed after the victory at Jericho and the devastating defeat at Ai.

In Joshua 7 the men of Ai route Joshua's army because of Achan, who took some devoted things rather than destroying them as God had commanded. As David Firth observes, "The story of Achan in Joshua 7 is in essence a mirror to the story of Rahab, where an Israelite who places his own wishes above those of Yahweh is effectively treated as a Canaanite. . . . This is a narrative where Canaanites become Israelites and Israelites become Canaanites, subverting expectations, with the key issue being whether or not there is wholehearted faithfulness to Yahweh."[27]

The theme of faithfulness to Yahweh as the basis of right standing with God returns in the story of Caleb the Kenizzite, a descendant of Esau. Caleb is the only other spy along with Joshua that brought back a good report to Moses (Num 13). God gives an inheritance in the promised land to Caleb, a non-Israelite, and to his daughter Achsah and their descendants (Josh 14:6–15; Judg 1:11–26). Rahab and Caleb aren't Israelites, "yet they (and perhaps others) were now part of Israel. Israel's identity is not ethnic, but finds ways to include the foreigner, with Rahab indeed as the paradigm figure for these chapters," as David Firth observes.[28]

The strict expectation that all the Canaanites must die or flee is reimagined, and the identity of Israelites is redefined to adapt to God's mission from the beginning and as promised to Abraham. By Joshua chapter 24, "there is no longer any mention of other nations, only other gods."[29] Actions done in faith to the Lord and abandonment of all other gods are the basis for right standing with God.

The Legacy of Rahab

Rahab changes our reading of the book of Joshua and the conquest of Canaan by upending our tendency toward an us-versus-them mentality. God places front and center a foreign woman with a demeaned reputation who demonstrates more integrity than the two spies or Achan. Rahab's faith, expressed in her words and actions, is honored by God. Her example displays the opportunity that awaits anyone in Canaan who will turn from allegiance to their gods and idols to align instead with Yahweh as the true and only God of gods and King of kings.

Like Shiphrah and Puah, the midwives of the exodus, Rahab is clever and outwits the king. Their boldness comes from their convictions. Like the midwives, Rahab shows that her faith in Yahweh exceeds her fear of human powers. "Rahab, just like Tamar and Miriam and Zipporah, and so many others, are not just accessories but primary instruments in God's plan for redemption as narrated in Scripture."[30]

In Joshua's encounter with the commander of the Lord's army, the Lord does not choose sides but asks, "Whose side are you on?" Each of us must decide if we are on the side of the prevailing or popular sociopolitical powers or if we are faithfully loyal to the Lord of lords, the all-wise creator God, demonstrated through our words and actions.

Joshua, who surely remembers his encounter with Rahab and with the commander of Yahweh's army, states toward the end of his life, "Now fear the LORD and serve him with all faithfulness. . . . But if serving the LORD seems undesirable to you, then choose for yourselves this day whom you will serve. . . . But as for me and my household, we will serve the LORD" (Josh 24:14–15).

Jesus spoke similar words: "No one can serve two masters. Either you will hate the one and love the other, or you will be devoted to the one and despise the other. You cannot serve both God and money" (Matt 6:24). This choice of who to serve lies before each of us every day.

The New Testament honors Rahab as well, naming her three times. First, she is named in the genealogy of Jesus, as the wife of Salmon, the mother of Boaz, who marries Ruth (Matt 1:5). Next in Hebrews 11:31: "By faith the prostitute Rahab, because she welcomed the spies, was not killed with those who were disobedient."[31] And James 2:23–25, which first quotes Genesis 15:6, "Abraham believed God, and it was credited to him as righteousness," goes on to say, "and he was called God's friend. You see that a person is considered righteous by what they do and not by faith alone. In the same way, was not even Rahab the prostitute considered righteous for what she did when she gave lodging to the spies and sent them off in a different direction?" Here, it is confirmed that Rahab's righteousness was obtained the same way as Abraham's: through faith in Yahweh.

> Like Tamar the Canaanite (Gen. 38), Jael the Kenite (Judges 4), and Ruth the Moabite (Ruth 1–4), Rahab becomes a model of faith and an ally to the people of God. In saving the Israelite spies, she humanizes the "other" and participates in carrying out Yahweh's divine plan. Rahab stands as a shining example of what is possible: a world in which those destined for destruction join the people of Israel in their worship of the one true God.[32]

Rahab's story speaks to all who have been unfaithful to God, which includes each of us. We can trust that God, who shows mercy to Rahab and her family, extends grace to us when we align our hearts with God's, speak and act in obedience to him, and allow him to transform our lives for his glory and our redemptive joy.

Reflect on the Chapter

* What reversals or surprises occur in the opening chapters of Joshua as God prepares the Israelites to enter the promised land? What does this reveal about God's heart and mission?
* How do Rahab's words and deeds demonstrate her faith in Yahweh?
* Describe Rahab and her family's experience of a Passover-type rescue. How are all of us saved through the "red cord" or the blood of the Passover lamb, which symbolizes the blood of Jesus, regardless of our past or our backgrounds?

Reflect on Your Life

* God weaved Rahab into the genealogy of Jesus. Can you identify anyone in your family tree who became a Christ follower? How has that affected your spiritual lineage?
* If you are the first in your family to become a Christ follower, how do you want to change the spiritual trajectory of your family?
* Has God's work in your life ever surprised you? If so, describe how God worked in unexpected ways and what you learned about him from that experience.

Take Your Bold Step

* Rahab boldly put her own life at risk by hiding and protecting the spies. What are some ways you can help those in your community who need protection or assistance?
* If there are people in your household who don't believe in Jesus yet, take some time to pray for them, and if there is an open door, share with them what God has done in your life.

Breath Prayer

(Inhale)   Yahweh, my God,

(Exhale)   I call upon your name.

CHAPTER 8

Deborah Leads, and Jael Drives the Victory Home

JUDGES 4–5

Deborah has the longest continuous narrative about a woman in the Bible other than the books of Ruth and Esther.* And rightly so. She is one of only three people in the Old Testament identified as both a judge and a prophet, along with Moses and Samuel. She is also the only woman to be called a "mother in Israel" (Judg 5:7).

Scripture and most rabbinic texts hold Deborah in high esteem "as an extremely righteous and praiseworthy woman."[1] The biblical text mentions "no negative traits in her [that other judges like Gideon and Samson had (Judg 6–8; 14–16)] such as making an ephod, doubting God's power, or taking personal vengeance on her enemies."[2]

The Jewish and Christian individuals who criticize her do so based on their cultural gender norms.[3] Some suggest that God made an exception in raising up Deborah as a leader because there were no good men available. For example, Wayne Grudem declares, "Something is abnormal, something is wrong—there are

---

* The narrative of Isaac finding Rebekah as a wife (Gen 24:15–67) is a close second in length, followed by Bathsheba (2 Sam 11:2–12:25 and 1 Kgs 1:11–37; 12:13–25) and Hannah's prayer for a child and dedication of Samuel (1 Sam 1:1–2:11).

no men to function as judge!"[4] Those uncomfortable with bold or effective women in Scripture debase her character as haughty, including in some rabbinic writings.[5] Others, such as Thomas Schreiner, minimize her role, suggesting that she handed her authority as a judge over to a man and that her prophetic work was exercised in private.[6]

To sift through these various views, we'll look carefully at the story of Deborah within the setting of the biblical story and then examine how she embodies the various titles she holds.

Deborah in the Cycle of the Judges

Deborah is introduced after three shorter narratives of the judges Othniel, Ehud, and Shamgar (Judg 3:7–31). After Ehud and Shamgar die, the Israelites again "did evil in the eyes of the LORD" (Judg 4:1). So the Lord again steps back and "sells" the Israelites into the hands of the local king of Canaan, Jabin, who oppresses and attacks them for twenty years.

The story of Deborah begins with the formula that typically introduces each judge in the book: the Israelites sin, Yahweh withholds his protection, an enemy army oppresses the people, the people cry out to Yahweh, and Yahweh delivers them through a judge (Judg 4:1–3). Deborah's story, however, is a slight departure from this formula.

Considering the pattern of Othniel and Ehud, the expectation is set that God will raise up a new judge to deliver Israel (Judg 3, 4:1–3). However, Deborah is presented first as a prophet, the wife of Lappidoth (or "a fiery woman," to be discussed later), and then as a woman already established as judging Israel "at that time." This distinguishes her from all the other cycles in Judges in which Yahweh raises up a judge to deliver the people.[7] In further contrast, Deborah sends for general Barak to come to her where she holds court, under the Palm of Deborah.

Who Is Deborah?

While the NRSVue translates Deborah's introduction "a prophet, wife of Lappidoth, was judging Israel" (Judg 4:4), another equally valid translation introduces her as "And Deborah, a woman who was a prophet—a woman of fire was she—she was judging Israel at that time" (Judg 4:4, translation by Susan Niditch).[8] She is the last judge in Judges upheld as an example of godliness and Yahweh-centeredness. Deborah, along with Jael the Kenite and Barak the Israelite general, brings Israel into victory and forty years of peace.

Deborah's name traditionally means "honeybee" but alternatively could be associated with a Hebrew word meaning "to lead or pursue."[9] Her tribe is uncertain. Considering the Song of Deborah, she may have been from the tribe of Issachar: "The princes of Issachar were with Deborah; yes, Issachar was with Barak" (Judg 5:15). Or considering the location where she sat at "the Palm of Deborah," she may have been a Benjaminite, or "more likely, an Ephraimite."[10]

She is also called "a mother in Israel" (Judg 5:7).

DEBORAH, A PROPHETESS

A prophet, or prophetess, is a person who speaks for God to their contemporaries through a vision, dream, or message.[11] The major named prophetesses in the Hebrew Bible are Miriam (Exod 15:20), Deborah (Judg 4:4), Isaiah's wife (Isa 8:3), Huldah (2 Kgs 22:14), and Noadiah (Neh 6:14). Deborah's authority is "based on her credibility as a true prophet, her presence at a site associated with oracular performance, and her ability to summon leaders to carry out the instructions of Yahweh."[12]

Deborah's role as prophet comes to the forefront when she informs Barak that Yahweh is commanding him to lead an Israelite army of ten thousand men against the forces of the

Canaanite king, Jabin (Judg 4:6–9).[13] She speaks with "authoritative words from a recognized seat of dispensing wisdom . . . as Moses had previously."[14]

She gives prophetic assurance that Yahweh will give the Canaanite army into Barak's hands (Judg 4:7), but Barak refuses to go to battle unless she goes with him. This is not to be interpreted as cowardice (Judg 4:8), for the testimony of Scripture through Samuel and the writer of Hebrews commend Barak as a faithful warrior and deliverer (1 Sam 12:11; Heb 11:32). Rather, in the face of the greatly superior military might of the Canaanite army, the "exchange between Barak and Deborah suggests the warrior's concern that no tribe would rally to his call without the presence of a divine representative."[15]

Deborah does not hesitate to go, demonstrating her confidence in Yahweh's word. But she prophetically declares, "Because of the course you are taking, the honor will not be yours, for the LORD will deliver Sisera [King Jabin's commander] into the hands of a woman" (Judg 4:9), to which Barak gives no argument. This is "a favorite theme of Judges and the larger Hebrew Bible concerning the victory of the unlikely hero. Sisera will be undone by a woman."[16]

Abraham Kuyper writes of her, "Deborah was mighty because the Spirit of the Lord, moved, qualified and inspired her. God kindled a fire in her heart. Sparks from it flew to all parts of Israel's hill-country. Heroic courage flared up in every heart. . . . Inspiring influences radiate from her and awaken the sleeping ones until such time as God shall cause the Light of His Christ to illuminate them."[17]

Kuyper draws his description in part from Deborah's next title.

DEBORAH, A WIFE, A FIERY WOMAN, OR BOTH?

The second identifier of Deborah in Judges 4:4 is an *'ēshet lappîdôt*, a phrase usually translated "wife of Lappidoth." If Lappidoth is her husband, the narrative oddly has nothing to say about him. Other scholars translate this as a "woman of flames," "fiery woman," "spirited woman," and "a woman of splendors"—descriptions that fit Deborah well.[18]

Notably, Barak means "lightning"—a name that parallels Deborah as "a woman of fire," as they work together to strike down the oppressor.[19]

Word play with dual meanings (double entendre) is a common and popular feature of biblical Hebrew. Therefore, she could be both a wife and a woman of fire. The word *lappid*, "torch," is a masculine singular noun that elsewhere has a masculine plural ending as *lappidim*.* But here in reference to Deborah, it has a uniquely feminine plural ending, *lappidoth* (especially unusual if referring to her husband's name).[20] Israelite listeners of this narrative "would have heard both meanings and would have enjoyed the play on words identifying independent, spirit-filled Deborah."[21]

DEBORAH, A JUDGE

Unlike the others in Judges, Deborah is not "raised up" for special service. Rather, the text tells us that she was already functioning as a judge.[22] "Repeatedly, Deborah speaks for Yhwh [Yahweh], even relaying his commands (הוצ), as did Moses, and offering authoritative words from a recognized seat of dispensing wisdom, namely, the Palm of Deborah, as Moses had previously" done, settling disputes and administering justice (Exod 18:13, 16).[23] Further, Deborah summons Barak to come to where she is serving, "by virtue of her official authority as judge."[24]

Deborah's wisdom earns her respect as a prophet and judge

---

* Alternate translations to "wife of Lappidoth" are based on the Hebrew grammar and word *lappid(im)* which is generally translated "torch(es)" in the Gideon and Samson story, and elsewhere (Judg 7:16, 20; 15:4; Gen 15:17; Isa 62:1; Ezek 1:13; Dan 10:6; Nah 2:4; and Zech 12:6), although the plural has the masculine ending in passages outside of Judg 4:4; see also, *HALOT*, 533.

of Yahweh. She fulfills "all the special duties of a judge, except that of military leader."[25] Traditionally, judges in Israel not only provided spiritual and legal leadership but also acted as military leaders in times of crisis. However, Deborah's role initially appears to exclude direct military leadership, as she focuses on her prophetic and judicial duties. This distinction shifts when Barak, the appointed military commander, hesitates to go into battle without her presence. At his request, Deborah steps into a leadership role on the battlefield, guiding the forces from Mount Tabor to the Kishon River.

DEBORAH, A MOTHER IN ISRAEL

From the Song of Deborah:

> The mountains quaked before the LORD, the One of Sinai,
> before the LORD, the God of Israel.
>
> "In the days of Shamgar son of Anath,
> in the days of Jael, the highways were
> abandoned;
> travelers took to winding paths.
> Villagers in Israel would not fight;
> they held back until I, Deborah, arose,
> until I arose, a mother in Israel." (Judg 5:5–7)

In the song, Yahweh is identified as "the God of Israel" in verse 5, and Deborah is identified as a mother in Israel in verse 7. These two verses are meant to be read together. Deborah is God's human representative, speaking on his behalf.[26] She is a woman who provides wise counsel and effective military advice to protect "the heritage of Yahweh," and she is aptly described as "a mother in Israel."[27]

She is the only woman in the Hebrew Bible referred to as a

"mother in Israel." The only other time "mother in Israel" appears is in reference to a city in northern Israel, Abel-beth-maacah (2 Sam 20:19). When David is facing a second rebellion after the near overthrow of his reign by Absalom his son, a troublemaker named Sheba takes David's deserters and flees to Abel. David's general Joab prepares to besiege Abel in pursuit of Sheba but is stopped by an unnamed wise woman who asks Joab if he will destroy the city of Abel, "a mother in Israel," part of "the LORD's inheritance" (2 Sam 20:19).

This wise woman in Abel negotiates with General Joab to have Sheba's head thrown over the city wall, thus saving the city from destruction.[28] The phrase "a city that is a mother in Israel," refers in part to "its geopolitical significance: *a city that is a mother in Israel* means one that has dependent villages called 'daughters.'"[29] Moreover, "a mother in Israel is one who brings liberation from oppression, provides protection, and ensures the well-being and security of her people."[30] Just as Abel is a city that is a mother in Israel, Deborah is a mother in the same sense. She, too, protects her people and looks after their well-being and security.

The Honor Goes to a Woman in Fulfillment of Deborah's Prophecy

In accordance with Deborah's prophecy that the Lord would deliver Sisera into the hands of a woman, Jael steps up and overturns the expectations of warfare. She is the wife of Heber the Kenite. The Kenites were Midianites, related to Jethro, Moses's father-in-law.[31] After Sisera's troops fall to Barak, Sisera flees to the Kenite compound since there is an alliance between King Jabin and Heber's family. Interestingly, Sisera heads straight to Jael's tent.* There is no mention of where her husband, Heber, is.

---

* It was common for the matriarch of the tribal family to have her own tent. See Genesis 24:67; see Cynthia R. Chapman, *The House of the Mother: The Social Roles of Maternal Kin in Biblical Hebrew Narrative and Poetry*, 1st ed. (New Haven, CT: Yale University Press, 2016).

We can surmise Jael's thoughts based on the inappropriateness of Sisera coming to her tent and the known exploitations of ancient Near Eastern warriors. As Claude Mariotti notes, "Although Sisera sought refuge among the Kenites, it was improper for a man to enter a woman's tent. (Judg 4:18) . . . Sisera's action was a violation of ancient Near Eastern traditions. Sisera's action was a violation of Heber's family and dishonored Jael by entering her tent. As a man, Sisera should have approached Heber and not his wife."[32]

When Jael sees Sisera coming to her tent, she invites him in, tucks him in with a blanket, gives him a skin full of milk, and he falls asleep. The phrase "Between her feet he sank, he fell, he lay" in Judges 5:27 (LEB) is laden with both sexual and birthing connotations in the Hebrew.[33]

This sexual language points to the plundering and raping of women that was assumed to occur by Sisera and his men, as the Song of Deborah graphically tells:

> Through the window peered Sisera's mother;
>> behind the lattice she cried out,
> "Why is his chariot so long in coming?
>> Why is the clatter of his chariots delayed?"
> The wisest of her ladies answer her;
>> indeed, she keeps saying to herself,
> "Are they not finding and dividing the spoils:
>> a woman or two [Hebrew, 'a womb or two] for
>>> each man,
> colorful garments as plunder for Sisera,
>> colorful garments embroidered,
> highly embroidered garments for my neck—
>> all this as plunder?" (Judg 5:28–30)

Michelle Knight comments fittingly about Jael:

The unconscionable devaluation of women to mere sexual/
reproductive organs (i.e., "wombs"; 5:30) reveals the extent to
which Jael's safety, let alone victory, was unexpected in the
context of war. Given this social perception, Jael is one further
example of how God chose those considered to be vulnerable,
exploitable, and unexpected to act as Israel's deliverers. This
socially vulnerable woman—whom Sisera's household might
have expected to be conquered in battles waged by the men
surrounding her—instead conquered the conqueror. [34]

Jael refuses to become a victim and raises up not just her
hand but a hammer and tent peg to assure Sisera's failure in making her another voiceless casualty of war along with those in the
region that he had oppressed for decades (Judg 4:1–3).[35]

The "Victory Song" of Deborah

"Victory song" is the most popular descriptor of the Song of
Deborah. Scholars consider the song among "the most ancient
writings in the Hebrew Bible."[36] Like the Song of Moses in
Deuteronomy 32 and the songs of Moses and Miriam in Exodus
15, the Song of Deborah in Judges 5 reminds the Israelites that
their God, who delivered them from slavery in Egypt, continues
to be at work in their midst.[37]

In Judges 5, Barak and Deborah join to sing the victory song
in unity.[38] The song mentions Deborah four times and Barak
three times. Barak is always mentioned in association with
Deborah, with him as a secondary figure. Even though they're
singing together, in 5:1 the verb is feminine singular, indicating
in Hebrew that she is the main singer. In 5:12 and 5:15, Deborah
is named before Barak.[39]

Yahweh, who continues to call his people to himself in covenant loyalty, shows and reminds his people that he rules over the

cosmos and all nature. God "empowers those considered lowly to accomplish great things. Earthly perceptions of power are senseless in the face of a God who fights for his people."[40] He does not require military might, but rather, trusting obedience to him, through which he brings an end to oppression and causes justice to prevail.

God's revelation in the book of Judges reaches its high point in the Song of Deborah.[41] The judges who follow Deborah, beginning with Gideon, misplace their confidence, beginning "a pattern of escalating deterioration among Israel's judges, who to greater and greater degrees relied on human means of securing victory—eventually setting a counterfeit king over themselves to fight their battles—rather than simply submitting to the only King who could ever save them."[42]

The Legacy of Deborah

God loves subverting human ideas of power and overturning our expectations, working through overlooked people in surprising ways to show himself strong. From the garden of Eden to the exodus, through the torah, warfare, and the prophets, Yahweh is seeking to make himself known (*yada*) as the faithful, covenant-keeping God.[43] Those who respond with loyal love to God he protects, guides, and blesses. Yahweh reveals himself consistently through his words and his actions in each of life's contexts and challenges.[44]

The respect or disrespect of women by men is a major component in the evaluation of the people in the book of Judges.[45] The way women are treated is an indication of the culture's relationship with God and one another. Male aggression and violence against women are contrary to God's vision of relationships of shalom. Genesis 1–11 sets the pattern and provides the lens through which to read the rest of Scripture, drawing a direct line between "male domination and violence" against women and "humanity's *rebellion against God.*"[46] God wants every society to take note and learn from these stories.

Deborah establishes an example of a woman in ministry as "a full-fledged prophetess, teaching and leading the people of Israel in a time of crisis."[47] She also sets an example for all of women as a "woman of fire," holding up a torch that drives out the darkness and drives out Israel's oppressors.

After Deborah, the nation steadily spirals downward with complete degradation of women into a military and moral morass until at the end of Judges everyone is doing what "was right in their own eyes" (Judg 21:25 NRSVue). Israel has become like Sodom. Yet hope remains.

God encourages us all to shine fervently, serving God brightly without holding back, unafraid to overturn limitations that mere people may impose when God says, "Arise!"

Reflect on the Chapter

* What titles did Deborah hold? How did she embody these designations?
* What do you think of Barak's refusal to go into battle unless Deborah accompanied him? What happened as a result?
* Dr. Faro writes that "God loves subverting human ideas of power and reversing expectations, working through overlooked people in surprising ways to show himself strong." How do you see God doing that in the story of Deborah, Barak, and Jael?

Reflect on Your Life

* Dr. Faro says that "the way women are treated is an indication of the culture's relationship with God and one another."

Do you agree with this statement, why or why not? Give examples from Scripture or from your experience.

* Deborah speaks with authority and confidently leads Israel in battle, which comes from her trust in God's word. Reflect on someone you know who lives and walks with the authority and confidence of God.

* How can you respond to God and his Word in a way that allows him to transform you so that you can speak, live, serve, and lead with more authority and confidence?

Take Your Bold Step

* Deborah was a bold leader. Not all of us hold positions of leadership, but we all have influence to lead others with wisdom that comes from God. What spheres of influence do you have? How can you wisely and intentionally use your influence in those areas for God's purposes?

* Deborah and Barak sang a song of praise to God after he gave them victory. What are some specific ways you can praise God for his faithfulness in your life? Take some time to write a song of praise.

Breath Prayer

(Inhale)   God, my Deliverer,
(Exhale)   I put my confidence in you.

CHAPTER 9

Ruth, a Woman of Valor and Loyal Love

THE BOOK OF RUTH

The book of Ruth is often presented as a love story between Boaz and Ruth. But that modern Hallmark movie version misses the plot and purpose of the book. Like the stories of Tamar, Rahab, and Jael, Ruth's story is about a reversal of expectations: God doing the unforeseen through the unexpected. Ruth, the destitute foreigner, emerges "as a character of extraordinary courage and nobility in her own right" through her guts, faith, and fortitude in the face of seemingly impossible odds.[1]

With God working behind the scenes, we witness once again how he is greater than our circumstances, no matter how dire. God shows up for the downtrodden and overlooked who have descended to the dregs of their dreams. In Ruth, what is empty becomes full through the tangible expression of loyal love, the Hebrew word *hesed*.

The Background to Ruth's Story

In the Old Testament, the book of Ruth is placed after Judges, which ends with Israel having become like Sodom, with everyone doing what is right in their own eyes (Judg 21:25). The book of

Ruth begins, "In the days when the judges ruled, there was a famine in the land" (Ruth 1:1). Because of the famine, a man from Bethlehem named Elimelek and his wife Naomi and two sons move to the land of Moab (east of the Dead Sea). Ironically, Bethlehem means the "House of Bread," but there is no bread, no food. What they thought would be a temporary relocation turns into ten years (Ruth 1:4).

While they wait for the famine to end, Elimelek dies and his two sons marry Moabite women. Then the two sons die, leaving Naomi with only her Moabite daughters-in-law, Orpah and Ruth. Orpah and Ruth are both childless. Within the first five verses of Ruth, we're left with the devastation of a family.

The significance of the famine cannot be overlooked. In Moses's final speech in Deuteronomy to the Israelites about to enter the promised land, God promises to bless his people with rain and abundance if they follow him and obey his words. But if they abandon God and serve other gods, then the land will not receive his blessing and will fail to produce crops. This is that time. Yet despite the Israelites' disobedience in the time of judges, Yahweh does not forsake his promises or fail to keep his covenant.

After ten years in Moab, Naomi hears that Yahweh has provided bread to his people. She rises to return to her hometown of Bethlehem. The word "return" repeats ten times in this first chapter, pointing to an upcoming turn of events for the family and the nation. By starting with the story of an ordinary family from Bethlehem, the chapter sets the stage to reveal "the unlikely origins of Israel's royal hope."[2]

Loyal Love (*Hesed*)

As Naomi rises to return home, the only possible future she foresees for her daughters-in-law is for them each to return to "your mother's home": for each to find a new husband. She urges them, saying, "May Yahweh show kindness [*hesed*] to you *just* as you did with the dead and with me" (Ruth 1:8 LEB). She introduces a key theological term through her blessing on Ruth and Orpah, the important Hebrew word *hesed*: Yahweh's covenant kindness, loyal love, grace, and faithfulness.[3]

Hesed is a core attribute of God, appearing twice when he declares who he is to Moses on Mount Sinai: "Yahweh, Yahweh, God, who is compassionate and gracious, slow to anger, and abounding with loyal love [*hesed*] and faithfulness, keeping loyal love [*hesed*] to the thousands . . ." (Exod 34:6–7 LEB). This word occurs over two hundred other places in the Hebrew Bible, including twenty-six times in the refrain of Psalm 136: "for his steadfast love [*hesed*] endures forever" (NRSVue).

God isn't the only one who can show *hesed*. People can too. Naomi beautifully identifies Ruth and Orpah's love as the same kind of loyal love as Yahweh's and expresses her hope that they will experience his covenantal kindness in return. This key word is used two more times in Ruth: to speak of Yahweh's *hesed* "to the living and the dead" shown through the words and actions of Boaz (Ruth 2:20); and of Ruth's *hesed* to Boaz (Ruth 3:10). Of the three times this word occurs in Ruth, twice it refers to Ruth's character.

In Daniel Block's commentary on Ruth, he provides a profound definition of love as a "covenant commitment demonstrated in action in the interests of the other person."[4] Only with this understanding can we frame the book of Ruth as a "love story" between Yahweh and his people and between people deeply committed to the well-being of those in their lives: family, foreigners, rich, and poor. It is a story of God demonstrating *hesed* love to his people, and people demonstrating *hesed* love to one another.

Ruth's Oath of *Hesed* Love

Ruth's loyal love is also expressed through her oath to Naomi at their lowest point.[5] In response to Naomi pressing Ruth to return to her Moabite home, we find Ruth's famous vow, often cited at weddings: "But Ruth replied, 'Don't urge me to leave you or to turn back from you. Where you go I will go, and where you stay I will stay. Your people will be my people and your God my God. Where you die I will die, and there I will be buried. May the LORD deal with me, be it ever so severely, if even death separates you and me'" (Ruth 1:16–17).

This oath required Ruth to leave her family and everything she knew in Moab to go to Israel, where she would be treated as an outcast. She knew that Naomi would not provide more sons for her. She knew that because she was a widow and a Moabite, life would be difficult for her in Israel. She had no obligation to stay with her mother-in-law. And yet she chose to make a vow of *hesed* love to Naomi, no matter how costly it would be for her.

Naomi relents only because of Ruth's determined *hesed*. The two women continue in silence to Bethlehem. They arrive to a swarm of women swirling with questions. Naomi can only muster a reply that expresses her anguish: "'Don't call me Naomi [which means *delightful*],' she told them. 'Call me Mara [which means *bitter*], because the Almighty has made my life very bitter. I went away full, but the LORD has brought me back empty. Why call me Naomi? The LORD has afflicted me; the Almighty has brought misfortune upon me'" (Ruth 1:20–21).

Naomi is so deep in her grief that she is not yet able to imagine goodness again. But Naomi left Bethlehem in a time of famine and returns in a time of harvest. Chapter 1 closes on a small but significant detail that they arrive "as the barley harvest was beginning" (1:22). Naomi does not know it yet; God's hidden provision will unfold through the barley harvest season and through

Ruth. As Marnie Legaspi observes, "The pain of her brokenness blinded her to Yahweh's care of her through the young woman standing beside her. Ruth was the beginning of her deliverance, yet she couldn't see it."[6]

The Unexpected Person of Valor (*Hayil*)

The second chapter of Ruth begins with the narrator informing us that Naomi has a relative in Bethlehem on her late husband's side by the name of Boaz. Boaz's father is Salmon, from the line of Judah. His mother is Rahab, the Canaanite prostitute who became the faithful follower of Yahweh and saved the Israelite spies in Jericho (Josh 2).

Boaz is introduced to us as an *ish gibbor hayil*, rendered in English as "a man of standing" (Ruth 2:1 NIV), "a prominent rich man" (LEB), or "a man of great wealth" (NASB). The Hebrew word *hayil* almost always describes men in terms of power, wealth, or property; or as upper class, noble, valiant; or as an army.[7] This word is used only three times in the Hebrew Bible in reference to a woman, as an *esheth hayil*. The phrase is found twice in Proverbs: "A wife of noble character is her husband's crown, but a disgraceful wife is like decay in his bones" (Prov 12:4); and "A woman of valour who can find? For her price is far above rubies" (Prov 31:10 JPS).

The third time *esheth hayil* occurs, it's spoken by Boaz to describe Ruth: "All the people of my town know that you are a woman of noble character [*esheth hayil*]" (Ruth 3:11). Significantly, Boaz calls Ruth a woman of valor not when she's a wife but when she is a poor and childless widow and a foreigner from an outcast nation, gleaning to keep her and Naomi alive.

It is no wonder and no mistake that in the Hebrew Bible, the book of Ruth is placed after Proverbs 31 (rather than after Judges, as it is in the English Bible), where a woman once identified only as a Moabite widow becomes recognized for who she truly is: a woman of noble character. Ruth becomes an emblem and encouragement for downtrodden women not to succumb to negative identities based on outward perceptions. Outwardly, she is on the bottom of society's social hierarchy, but God looks at the heart and tells us to do the same.

The Hidden Provision of Yahweh's *Hesed* at Work

Naomi and Ruth arrive in Bethlehem during the barley harvest destitute and without a plan. Naomi, as Gene Tucker puts it, "wasn't even in a place where she could accept help.... [Like many trauma victims,] Naomi had a number of basic needs that needed to be met before she could begin to hope and care again."[8] Ruth, however, rises up to do what she can. She says to Naomi, "Let me go to the fields and pick up the leftover grain behind anyone in whose eyes I find favor" (Ruth 2:2). Sometimes just doing what we can (which may not seem like much) is the biggest step of faith.

In ancient Israel, "Gleaning the land's leftovers was an institutionalized social practice to provide for the most vulnerable and impoverished in the community: the alien, orphan, and widow (Lev. 19:9–10; 23:22; Deut. 24:19)."[9] And "she just happened to end up in the portion of the field belonging to Boaz, who was from the clan of Elimelech" (Ruth 2:3 NET). What feels like happenstance in the moment, we later recognize as God's gentle guiding hand.

Boaz sees the new young woman gleaning in his field and asks his overseer about her. He is told she's the Moabite who returned with Naomi. He knows her story and that she's a close relative. He takes action to protect her safety and provide food for her and Naomi (Ruth 2:5–16). Ruth doesn't discover his relationship to them until she returns home. Naomi immediately informs her, "That man is our close relative; he is one of our guardian-redeemers [*go'el*]" (Ruth 2:20). A glimmer of hope rises up in Naomi.

The convergence of goodness in three forms opens the way for this breath of hope: a good law of the land (the opportunity to glean); a good woman of bravery (Ruth); and a good man of influence (Boaz, who doesn't take advantage of Ruth's vulnerability but protects her). Ultimately, the people of Bethlehem and the readers of the Bible recognize God's *hesed* in his orchestration of the time, place, and people to provide for Ruth and Naomi and continue the redemptive narrative of Scripture.

The second chapter ends with Ruth living with Naomi while she continues gleaning through the barley and the wheat harvests. This season would have lasted about five months, from March through July. But Naomi must have wondered how they would survive after the wheat harvest was over.

Responsibility of the Kinsman-Redeemer (*Go'el*)

In the first chapter of Ruth, Naomi tells her daughters-in-law that she has no more sons to provide for them to continue the family line. The levirate law in Israel "designates the duty of a man to marry the sonless widow of his deceased brother."[10] If there is no *levir* (or brother-in-law), the broader term *go'el* applies.

A *go'el*, often translated into English as "kinsman-redeemer" or simply "redeemer," is "the male relative of a deceased, who leaves a childless widow behind" and is responsible for her well-being, "to **redeem** her from childlessness through marriage" (Ruth 2:20; 3:9, 12; 4:1, 3, 4, 6, 8, 14).[11] Since the levirate law requiring a son-in-law to marry his brother's wife does not apply in Naomi and Ruth's case, "the law of redemption" through the *go'el* (Lev 25:25–28) must apply.[12] The *go'el* is responsible to redeem and assist the "impoverished relatives during times of hardship."[13]

Boaz knows he is a *go'el*, a kinsman-redeemer, yet months pass and neither he nor any other relative of Elimelek steps up to take responsibility for Naomi and Ruth. Possibly we can give Boaz the excuse that Naomi can no longer bear a child, so there's no point marrying her. And possibly, because Boaz is considerably older than Ruth (Ruth 2:8; 3:10), he assumes Ruth would not want to marry him. So he gives Ruth safe gleaning and extra grain but has no conversation with either Naomi or Ruth about his responsibility as a possible kinsman-redeemer.

Naomi and Ruth's situation requires creative measures to bring about their wholeness and restore Elimelek's family line. Daniel Block writes, "Since he [Boaz] was obviously not making a move, Naomi took it upon herself to overcome his inertia."[14] Naomi's rising hope overcomes her bitterness and prompts her bold instructions to Ruth.

A Bold Betrothal (Finding Refuge Under His Wings)

Now that both the barley and wheat harvest are complete, it's threshing time in Bethlehem. Who knows what the next source of food might be for Naomi and Ruth, or when they might have an opportunity to speak privately with Boaz regarding his potential responsibility as their redeemer? Neither Naomi nor Ruth knows whether Boaz is willing to step up to provide as their family redeemer.

The next step Naomi and Ruth take is controversial! On threshing day, Naomi tells Ruth to wash up, anoint herself with oil, put on her dress, and go to the threshing floor at night when everyone is done for the day and finished eating and drinking. She further instructs Ruth to hide until she sees where Boaz lies down, and then after he's asleep to "uncover his feet and lie down. He will tell you what to do" (Ruth 3:4).

Is Naomi's suggestion to Ruth scandalous? Is Ruth going to Boaz as a temptress, as some scholars have argued?[15] Or is Naomi telling Ruth to privately prompt Boaz to take responsibility as their family redeemer since, so far, he's made no such move?

Three significant determinants argue against this act being scandalous: the character of Ruth and Boaz; Ruth's use of the language "spread your wings over me since you are a kinsman-redeemer" (Ruth 3:9, my translation); and the clarity of their conversation and subsequent actions.[16]

First, Ruth is consistently shown as a woman of noble character: she's loyal and respectful. So much so that the entire town of Bethlehem holds her in high regard. Boaz is likewise consistently portrayed as a man of noble character, showing respect and care for Ruth, all his workers, and those around him.

When Boaz first meets and speaks to Ruth, he calls her "my daughter" (2:8), using the same term as Naomi when she speaks to Ruth. He urges her to continue to glean in his field, where she will be safe, and to drink water with his workers. He continues to give extra food and portions to Ruth and Naomi. Boaz greets his workers with, "The LORD be with you," and they reply, "The LORD bless you" (Ruth 2:4). His conversation with his overseer is relaxed, and he instructs his workers to treat Ruth safely. The text indicates that the women who work for Boaz in his fields are also expected to be treated with respect by his male workers, because Boaz tells Ruth to work alongside the women and not to go to the fields of another property owner, where her safety is not assured. The safety of the women working for Boaz is assured.

Second, Ruth is first described by Boaz as having "come to take refuge under the wings [*kanaf*] of Yahweh" (Ruth 2:12, my translation). We see this in their first conversation, after Ruth asks him why she has found favor in his eyes. Boaz replied, "I've been told all about what you have done for your mother-in-law since the death of your husband—how you left your father and mother and your homeland and came to live with a people you did not know before. May the LORD repay you for what you have done. May you be richly rewarded by the LORD, the God of Israel, under whose wings [*kanaf*] you have come to take refuge" (Ruth 2:11–12).

The last phrase—"under whose wings you have come to take refuge"—is very similar to the middle line of Psalm 91:4, speaking of Yahweh's protection of those who trust in him: "Under his wings you will find refuge." The symbol of a bird spreading its wings is associated with deliverance by Yahweh (Deut 32:11; Jer 48:40; 49:22). The word for "wings" in Hebrew also refers to the corner or hem of a garment (e.g., 1 Sam 15:27; 24:4 [in Hebrew, 24:5] and 24:11 [in Hebrew, 24:12]).[17]

When one understands the social structure of ancient Israel, it's not surprising that the same language is used of a marriage proposal. Adele Berlin notes, "When Boaz awakes, startled to find Ruth at his feet, she asks him to spread his robe over her—a symbolic act of espousal—because Boaz is a 'redeeming kinsman,' that is, one who has a right to redeem Elimelech's property and at the same time to marry his son's widow so as 'to perpetuate the name of the deceased upon his estate' (Ruth 4:5)."[18]

Gale Yee affirms "that Ruth is proposing marriage to Boaz, as well as asking for his protection" when she lies down at his feet, under the "wings" or hem of his garment (see also Ezek 16:8; Ruth 3:4, 7–8).[19]

Jean-Louis Ska points out that Ruth's initiative is the "turning point" of the plot, setting Boaz in motion.[20] Yes, the man was expected to act first. Boaz could have, or should have, come to Naomi as a family redeemer and asked for Ruth in marriage. But Ruth's bold action and words, as Daniel Block observes, "immediately subverted this social order by lecturing Boaz on his obligations. Accepting the lecture, Boaz declared in effect that he was the servant of Ruth, the destitute Moabite widow!"[21]

Third, Ruth, while taking a brave step, wisely defers to Boaz by calling herself his servant. And Boaz, unlike Lot in Genesis 19, is not portrayed as being in a drunken stupor, but rather merely being asleep and then awakened, shocked to find someone at his feet. He engages in intelligent dialogue and expresses concern for Ruth's reputation and safety.

Boaz identifies Ruth's well-established character as an *esheth hayil*, a woman of valor (Ruth 3:11). He then asks for her shawl, or outer garment (note that she is fully dressed, including an outer cloak), and he fills it with grain. Upon returning home, Ruth conveys to Naomi everything Boaz has done for her. Naomi then tells Ruth that "the man will not rest until the matter is settled today" (Ruth 3:18), which shows her trust in Boaz's noble character. When day breaks, Boaz immediately gets to work on fulfilling her request for marriage and taking his responsibility as the kinsman-redeemer.

Boaz steps in as an image bearer of God, reflecting God as our ultimate Redeemer. As Robert Hubbard observes, "In essence, the human kinsman carries out the redemption policy of the 'Great Kinsman,' Yahweh himself. One might even say that the human kinsman personally represents Yahweh in such transactions."[22]

Then Comes Marriage, Then Comes a Baby . . . in the Line of David

In the final chapter of Ruth, Boaz leaves the threshing floor and proceeds to the city gate to conduct the business at hand. A closer kinsman-redeemer to Naomi happens to pass by. This is the third time the narrator discreetly refers to an event happening, as the Hebrew implies, seemingly by chance (Ruth 2:4; 3:8; 4:1), to which Block attests that "a deeper hearing recognizes again the hidden hand of God."[23]

Naomi's emptiness is filled as Ruth finds "rest" in the home of her husband. The elders and women speak blessings over them. The story continues with a birth narrative similar to those used of Sarah and Isaac (Gen 18:9–15) and Hannah and Samuel (1 Sam

1:1–20) when a barren woman gives birth to a child of special importance to the nation. God is portrayed "as an actor in the drama by granting Ruth conception, though as in 1:6 [through the news of food in Bethlehem], he acted behind the scenes."[24] The women of the town praise God for not leaving Naomi without a kinsman-redeemer: "For your daughter-in-law, who loves you and who is better to you than seven sons, has given him birth" (v. 15).

Remarkably, Ruth, this Moabite widow who made a vow to Naomi and demonstrated bold *hesed* action, is recognized by the whole community as better than seven sons!

The book of Ruth culminates with a short genealogy of David, beginning with Perez, the son of Judah and Tamar: "Now these are the descendants of Perez: Perez fathered Hezron, and Hezron fathered Ram, and Ram fathered Amminadab, and Amminadab fathered Nahshon, and Nahshon fathered Salmon, and Salmon fathered Boaz, and Boaz fathered Obed, and Obed fathered Jesse, and Jesse fathered David" (Ruth 4:18–22).

This genealogy points to the ultimate kinsman-redeemer, Jesus, who will come through the line of David.

Ruth's Legacy

Ruth's name is included in Matthew's genealogy of Jesus (Matt 1:5), which is significant because women do not appear in most ancient Jewish genealogies. Moreover, no other book of the Old Testament is named after a non-Israelite, and only one of two books in the Bible are named for a woman.

Rahab and Ruth form a kind of frame around Joshua and Judges. In a time of instability, God was trying to establish his "kingdom of priests" in the promised land among his often less than faithful people (Exod 19:6). Yet Scripture places a Canaanite woman in Jericho and a Moabite woman in Bethlehem at the beginning and the end of the narratives (Josh 2; Ruth). Rahab and

Ruth stand out as faithful believers and followers of Yahweh, each joined by marriage to men from the tribe of Judah, who become matriarchs to the line of the Messiah. They are each an *ezer* and a *tsela* (see chapter 2, "Man and Woman as Sacred Space").

Carolyn Custis James maintains that "a woman's high calling as God's image bearer renders her *incapable* of insignificance, no matter what has gone wrong in her life or how much she has lost. Even if her community shoves her aside, turns a deaf ear to the sound of her voice, or regards her as invisible—even if she is forced into a passive role in her community—she remains vital to God's purposes and is a solid contributor anyway. She cannot be stopped."[25]

In the story of Ruth, we find God is present, actively working behind the scenes, in the restoration of a devastated family through people who demonstrate loyal love when the path forward seems lost. Ruth faced great uncertainty as a childless widow in a foreign land with no foreseeable help, but through loyal love and bold commitment, she stands out as a woman of valor. Sometimes faith is trusting God when we can't see the way or hear his voice. Sometimes God leads in obscurity and asks us to get up and do what we can with what we have. Sometimes the greatest step of faith is into the unknown, knowing only that Yahweh's *hesed* will never cease to be present for his people.

Reflect on the Chapter

* The Hebrew word *hesed* is a recurring theme throughout the book of Ruth. What does *hesed* mean, and who demonstrates *hesed* in the book of Ruth?
* Where do you see God working behind the scenes to provide for Ruth and Naomi?
* Boaz calls Ruth a woman of valor, or *eshet hayil*. The women in the town also tell Naomi that Ruth is better than seven

sons. Describe what it means to be a woman of valor and how Ruth demonstrates this.

Reflect on Your Life

* In the beginning of the book of Ruth, Naomi is so blinded by grief that she can't see the goodness of God's provision in the person right beside her. It takes her a while to renew her hope and eventually recognize God's guiding hand in her life. Describe a time when God was providing for you but you couldn't see it. Or describe how you see God's provision in your life right now.

* When Ruth and Naomi move to Bethlehem, they don't know how they will make ends meet. Ruth does the next thing she thinks of, which is to glean the edges of a field. If you are experiencing uncertainty in your life, what is the one next step you can take?

Take Your Bold Step

* At their lowest point, Ruth boldly vows to be committed to Naomi. Naomi hatches a bold plan that will provide for Ruth and their family line. Is there someone in your life for whom you can take bold, and perhaps even selfless, action to support their well-being? For example, perhaps God is prompting you to make a commitment to be a loyal friend or provide financially for a loved one in need.

Breath Prayer

(Inhale)   Jesus, my Redeemer,
(Exhale)   guide my steps.

CHAPTER 10

Hannah's Prayer Changes History

1 SAMUEL 1–2

After the downward spiral toward the end of Judges, 1 Samuel opens with a ray of hope through the story of Hannah. Because of her plight, her prayer, and her promise, God grants her a son, Samuel, who reforms the priesthood and births the monarchy in Israel.[1] Hannah's name comes from the Hebrew word *hen*, meaning "favor, grace."[2] Through her, favor and grace come to the nation of Israel.

During the time of the judges, the people were in desperate straits. Forty years after Deborah and Barak's victory, the majority of the Israelites no longer knew their God, Yahweh, and no longer served him.[3] The tribes descended into a moral morass until they became like Sodom and Gomorrah.

Hannah's story resets the expectation of the Israelites to move toward the hope that a godly king will establish order and fruitfulness for the people God miraculously delivered from slavery in Egypt and settled in the promised land.

Hannah's Story Within the Bible

With the introduction of Hannah, we're reminded that every miracle begins with a need. Her story connects with the intricate interweaving of multiple motifs we've encountered so far. The books of Genesis through Kings are intended to be read as a continuous "unified narrative."[4]

From Genesis onward we find the theme of "God's intervention in overcoming the barrenness of the matriarchs."[5] Each of the barren-mother narratives leads to the birth of a son who becomes an important figure in salvation history: Sarah gives birth to Isaac (Gen 11:29–30; 16:1–18; 21:1–2), Rebekah gives birth to Jacob (Gen 25:20–34;), Rachel gives birth to Joseph (Gen 30:1, 22–24), Samson's mother gives birth to Samson (Judg 13:2, 24), Hannah gives birth to Samuel (1 Sam 1:2, 20), and Elizabeth gives birth to John the Baptist (Luke 1:7). Each of these incorporate elements of divine and human initiatives significant to "the ongoing story of divine guidance to Israel."[6]

From Exodus we continue the theme of overlooked women who become deliverers by refusing to give up hope for descendants, even under harsh circumstances and overlords.* Hannah lives during the chaotic times of the judges when Canaanites, Midianites, Philistines, and Moabites oppressed the land. Yet she, like Jochebed, who lived in a time when Israelites were oppressed by the Egyptians, preserves the life of a baby whom God raises up to save the Israelites. Both Jochebed and Hannah raise their own sons until they are weaned, then hand them over in faith to another to raise for their future calling. As Jochebed's son Moses establishes a nation, Hannah's son Samuel establishes a dynasty.

From Joshua we continue the theme of the faithful outsider.

---

* This theme begins in Genesis with Eve, who bears Seth (Gen 4:1, 25–26), and Tamar, who bears Perez and Zerah (Gen 38).

The Canaanite Rahab's faith in Yahweh exceeds that of the two Israelite spies. Her faithfulness also far surpasses the disobedience of unfaithful Achan of the clan of Judah (Josh 2:1–24; 7:1–26). The faith of the barren and taunted Hannah exceeds the faith of Eli the priest. And the faithfulness of her son Samuel far exceeds the unfaithfulness of Eli's priestly sons Hophni and Phinehas. Rescued Rahab marries into the tribe of Judah. Rahab's son Boaz and Ruth become the great-grandparents of King David. Thus, Rahab's and Hannah's futures intersect when Hannah's elderly son Samuel anoints Rahab's great-great-grandson, the young David, as king.

From Judges we continue the theme of divinely appointed deliverers and prophets. Hannah's prophetic song is likened to Deborah's and much later to Mary's Magnificat. Both Deborah and Hannah confront a top leader: Deborah summons general Barak into military action; Hannah corrects priest Eli's scorn, which evokes him into blessing her prayerful vow to Yahweh. Hannah's son Samuel joins Moses and Deborah as the only three named in Scripture as judge and prophet of Yahweh. Hannah's prophetic song foretells her son's role in ushering in the monarchy that Moses earlier foretold (Deut 17:14–20; 1 Sam 2:1–10; 16:13).

From Ruth we find the connection between Naomi's suffering and Hannah's "bitterness" of soul. The women of Bethlehem declare that Ruth is worth seven sons, while Hannah's husband asks if he isn't worth ten sons (Ruth 4:15; 1 Sam 1:8). To both, God brings the grace and fulfillment of an heir.

Hannah's story also bears the theme of the "silent sufferer" from Tamar in Genesis 38, which carries forward into the story of Bathsheba.[7] After years of silence, these women find and use their voices, which effects change in the monarchy and transforms history. Tragically, not all the women who are silenced and trodden upon are heard. When their voices are ignored, great harm comes to the families of the leaders who silenced them—and sometimes to the nation. The silent sufferers ultimately foreshadow the coming of the suffering servant who bears the grief and pain of the world, who will return again with a great shout of victory.

Hannah's Plight

The books of Samuel begin with the lineage of a man, Elkanah, but swiftly turn attention to his two wives, Hannah and Peninnah. As with the introduction of Abram and Sarai, we are immediately informed that this is a barren-wife story, signaling that God has extraordinary purposes in store (Gen 11:27–30).

As we saw with Sarah and Tamar, a woman without an heir was vulnerable to being replaced or shamed. A wife's identity and value were tied to her motherhood. The ability to produce an heir was essential to prevent the extinction of the family line.

Elkanah is a religious man and takes his family on an annual pilgrimage to worship and give sacrificial offerings to "the LORD of hosts at Shiloh" (1 Sam 1:3 NRSVue). As Isaac loved Rebekah and Jacob loved Rachel, we're told that Elkanah loved Hannah (Gen 24:67; 29:18; 1 Sam 1:5). So Peninnah seems to be the secondary wife of Elkanah, added to produce children in lieu of barren Hannah.

Twice in two verses it's stated that Yahweh closed Hannah's womb (1 Sam 1:5–6). Because of this, Peninnah, the rival wife, persists in provoking her. Elkanah tries ineffectively to comfort Hannah with questions that hurt rather than help. Hannah is voiceless, grieved to her core, after years of vicious taunting by Peninnah for her failure to produce children. "This went on year after year. Whenever Hannah went up to the house of the LORD, her rival provoked her till she wept and would not eat. Her husband Elkanah would say to her, "Hannah, why are you weeping? Why don't you eat? Why are you downhearted? Don't I mean more to you than ten sons?" (1 Sam 1:7–8).

But Elkanah doesn't attempt to stop Peninnah's cruelty, as

Eli, the priest doesn't attempt to correct his sons' wickedness. The "obtuseness that we see in both Elkanah and (later) Eli seems typical of the attitudes of the men of the time (and indeed of many times) towards women, but the writer, almost certainly a man, is able to observe, present and critique that obtuseness."[8]

HANNAH AROSE AND PRAYED

But this year is different for Hannah. This year, Hannah "arose" (NKJV), which uses the same verb (*qwm*) as in Deborah's Song when she "arose, a mother in Israel!" (Judg 5:7; 1 Sam 1:9). "Hannah's arising puts her in the company of Rebekah, Tamar, Deborah, Naomi and Ruth, Abigail, Esther, and the proverbial valiant woman in Proverbs, all women who rise up and tackle formidable and at times daring tasks (Gen 24:61; 38:19; Judg 4:9; Ruth 1:6; 2:15; 3:14; 1 Sam 25:41–42; Esth 8:5; Prov 31:15)."[9]

Hannah arises, overwhelmed by the bitterness of her soul, and she goes and stands near the doorpost of the temple where Eli is sitting. She prays silently to Yahweh while still weeping in deep lament.[10] She vows to the Lord of hosts (or Lord of armies, the warrior God), saying, "If you will only look on your servant's misery and remember me, and not forget your servant but give her a son [Hebrew, a "seed"], then I will give him to the LORD for all the days of his life, and no razor will ever be used on his head" (1 Sam 1:11).[11] Hannah is the only woman in the Old Testament who makes and keeps a vow. Her husband, thankfully, does not try to deter her or nullify her vow.[12]

Hannah remains in earnest prayer, silently weeping and mouthing her words. Significantly, her heartfelt prayer, offered while standing and moving only her lips, becomes a model for Jewish prayer practices. The Amidah, the primary element of the Jewish daily prayer is done while standing, the person silently mouthing the words with deep intent. "It is from Hannah that Jews learn to practice one of the most important of Jewish prayers."[13]

The priest Eli, however, assumes she is drunk. His response speaks to the times: "How long are you going to stay drunk? Put away your wine" (1 Sam 1:14). "The suspicion of the aged priest seems to indicate that the vice of intemperance was neither uncommon nor confined to one sex in those times of disorder."[14]

This time Hannah speaks up.

"Not so, my lord," Hannah replies. "I am a woman who is deeply troubled. I have not been drinking wine or beer; I was pouring out my soul to the LORD. Do not take your servant for a wicked woman [Hebrew, *bath-beliyyaal,* "daughter of worthlessness," or, *belial*]; I have been praying here out of my great anguish and grief" (1 Sam 1:15–16). Ironically, the word *belial* that she uses to describe Eli's assumption about her is what God later calls Eli's two sons. "The full import of her spirited retort is lost on us till the next mention of Eli's sons (2:12); they are 'Sons of No Use,' but she denies being a 'Daughter of No Use.'"[15]

Being corrected, Eli recognizes his error and says, "Go in peace, and may the God of Israel grant you what you have asked of him" (1 Sam 1:17). Eli's words can be understood as prophetic, that is, "the God of Israel *will* grant . . ."—an expression of confidence that God will answer.[16] Hannah responds (whether to Eli or to Yahweh is uncertain), "May your servant find favor [*hen*] in your eyes" (1 Sam 1:18).[17] After pouring out her heart and receiving Eli's blessing, she walks away, eats food, and is no longer sorrowful. The next morning, Elkanah's family awakes, worships before Yahweh, and returns to their home in Ramah.

GOD REMEMBERS HANNAH

Once home, Hannah does her part: she and Elkanah make love, and God does his part: "the LORD remembered her" (1 Sam 1:19). The Lord who initially "closed her womb" (v. 6) now "remembered her" (v. 19), and she conceives and bears a son.

In the Old Testament, to "remember" someone is not simply to think about them or to recall something once forgotten but to act on their behalf. When God "remembered Noah" (Gen 8:1), he began to reverse the flood waters. When God heard the groanings of the Israelites in slavery in Egypt, he "remembered" his covenant with Abraham, Isaac, and Jacob and raised up Moses as their deliverer (Exod 2:24).

Hannah names her son Samuel because "I asked the LORD for him" (1 Sam 1:20). Samuel's name is a play on words.[18] His name sounds somewhat like the Hebrew root word *sha'al* ("to ask"), but a more straightforward translation of Samuel is "name of God," or "God is his name." Similarly, the future king Saul's name means "asked of God," for the people ask God for a king. Not surprisingly, the names and lives of both Samuel and Saul are intertwined in the biblical story and in their destinies.[19]

HANNAH'S PROMISE

At the family's next annual pilgrimage to worship in Shiloh, Hannah does not go. Rather, she tells her husband that after Samuel is weaned, she will "take him and present him before the LORD, and he will live there always" (1 Sam 1:22). Elkanah simply responds to Hannah, "Do what seems best to you" and agrees to her plan (v. 23).

We're not told how long Hannah nurses young Samuel, but weaning generally occurred around age three.[20] After he is weaned, Hannah and Elkanah bring young Samuel to the house of Yahweh at Shiloh with a three-year-old bull,* flour, and wine for

---

* The Masoretic Text (MT) reads "three bulls," but the Dead Sea Scrolls, Septuagint, and Syriac read "three-year-old bull." Further, verse 25 in the MT and others refers to the sacrifice of a "bull" in the singular. The NRSV, NIV, CSB and others have gone with "three-year-old bull." See also Bryan E. Beyer, "1 Samuel," in *CSB Study Bible: Notes*, 413, which suggests that one bull was set aside for a sacrifice of thanksgiving for Samuel's birth and the other two were part of Elkanah's usually annual sacrifice.

their sacrifice (v. 24). After they worship and offer their sacrifices, they bring their son to Eli.

Hannah politely reminds Eli of their previous encounter, her intercessory prayer, and Eli's words. Then Hannah informs Eli, "'I prayed for this child, and the LORD has granted me what I asked of him. So now I give him to the LORD. For his whole life he will be given over to the LORD.' And he worshiped the LORD there" (vv. 27–28). Eli likewise does not object but agrees to her vow and receives the small boy into his home.

After years of suffering in silence, once Hannah speaks, the men respect her godliness, offer no objections, and agree to her decisions.

In the opening two chapters of 1 Samuel, five times Hannah makes prayers of intercession, with the last mention introducing Hannah's Song (1 Sam 1:10, 12, 26, 27; 1 Sam 2:1).* The only other person noted in 1 Samuel to make prayers of intercession is Samuel, and later, David in 2 Samuel (1 Sam 7:5; 8:6; 12:19, 23; 2 Sam 7:27).

Samuel is raised up in Shiloh under Eli, in service to Yahweh. Each year when Hannah and Elkanah make their annual sacrifice in Shiloh, she brings her son a new linen priestly robe. In fulfillment of Eli's blessing upon the couple, Hannah has three more sons and two daughters. "Meanwhile, the boy Samuel grew up in the presence of the LORD" (1 Sam 2:21).

Hannah, whose faith influenced her son Samuel, stands in stark contrast to Eli, who refuses to train or correct his own sons' evil actions. Yet Eli does train Samuel to hear and respond to the voice of Yahweh. As foretold, Eli's two sons die in battle. When Eli hears the news, he falls over and also dies. But Samuel continues to grow in wisdom and favor, transforming the priesthood and obeying Yahweh as king, even when the people rebel (1 Sam 2:26–8:21).

---

* The word "prayer" in 1 Samuel 2:1 occurs in the Masoretic Text but not in the Septuagint.

Hannah's Song

The Song of Hannah stands alongside "the songs of Miriam, Deborah, and the Virgin Mary, as well as those of Moses, David, Hezekiah, and other psalmists and prophets."[21] Her song sets the trajectory in 1 and 2 Samuel for the prophetic foretelling and approval of the monarchy her son will install.[22]

Hannah's Song is one of four songs, or poetic prayers, that frame the two books of Samuel. The other three are David's lament over the death of Saul and Jonathan at the beginning of 2 Samuel (2 Sam 1:19–27), the Song of David (2 Sam 22:2–51, which is also Psalm 18), and the last poetic words of David (2 Sam 23:1–7) near the close of 2 Samuel.[23] The importance of Hannah's Song in 1 Samuel is not fully seen until the end of 2 Samuel, when the outworking of her prophetic utterances has been realized and echoed in David's psalm.

Cheryl You notes, "As bookends to the books of Samuel, Hannah and David's songs (and their stories) reveal that God works through the reversal of fortunes, humbling the lofty and elevating the weak."[24] Yet it is Hannah's "powerful determination to overcome adversity" that "places her at the forefront of the compelling narrative."[25]

Hannah's Song declares that there is no one holy like Yahweh, no rock like our God; he raises the lowly from the dust and the needy from the ash heap (garbage dump). He reverses fortunes and upends the status quo so that the humble might trust in him and the proud be brought low.

Her prophetic song is echoed in Mary's Magnificat, which "extols Yhwh's power to bring down the mighty and raise the lowly. Yet in contrast to the Magnificat, it also concludes by praising the strength that Yhwh 'will give his king,' reflecting Hannah's premonition that her son will be closely involved in the rise of the nation's monarchy."[26]

The song begins and ends with triumph! As Hebrew scholar Michael Fishbane notes, it anticipates Samuel's anointing of David as king with a horn of oil, which "takes on a messianic tone of promise."[27] In Jewish liturgy, Hannah's Song is the basis for the standard daily Jewish prayer, the Amidah, which asks the Lord to "cause the Branch of David Your servant to sprout" and to "raise up his horn with Your salvation."[28]

Hannah's Legacy

Through Hannah's story, God once again demonstrates his strategic placement of women to initiate key movements in salvation history. Through their silence, words, prayers, songs, and actions, women "become foils to errant male leadership . . . calling leadership to account and reminding them of who they are supposed to be."[29] Those who pay attention recognize that women placed by God, even in seemingly obscure roles, bring reformation and transformation. Those who ignore godly women do so to their personal, familial, or national peril.

God's work in human history often begins with a void, an emptiness, a need. Sometimes his work begins in the midst of oppression that is felt deeply by seemingly insignificant people. As Mary Evans writes,

> The books of Samuel as a whole present a series of power-struggles between those men who are seen as the most significant figures within the nation. But we begin with the story of a barren woman whose childlessness leaves her powerless even within her own family situation. It seems certain that this is a deliberate attempt to encourage the reader to think further about life, about the significance of individuals and about what real power is.[30]

Hannah, though powerless to change her situation on her own, poured out her heart and appealed to the One who has real power. In time she "arose" in God's strength. In Hannah's Song (1 Sam 2:1) she says, "In the LORD my horn is lifted high"—"horn" meaning strength. God works powerfully by filling the void of her power with his own.[31]

In Hannah's story, we see how God can work through even the most personal and profound longings. Even when those longings are beyond human ability to fulfill, God can meet the desire of the aching who call out to him in faith. God can be at work through our deepest desires. As Old Testament scholar Koowon Kim writes,

> Hannah did not go to the temple with the intention of shaping Israel's history. However, when she responded with faith to her personal problem, the Lord used her faith to change the course of Israel's history. We learn from this that our everyday efforts to live out our faith matter in the kingdom of God. We do not need to be famous pastors or theologians or even politicians or scientists to make a difference in this fallen world that needs divine intervention. God uses our little acts of faith for his great purpose.[32]

Our response to taunting, barrenness, oppression, and shaming carries consequences that extend far beyond what we can comprehend. Hannah's heartfelt prayer and unwavering trust in God not only brought the fulfillment of her desire for a child but also set the stage for a greater purpose. Through the birth of Samuel, a prophet who would anoint kings and guide Israel, God demonstrated how he works through the lowly and the overlooked to bring deliverance and blessing. What may seem like a private struggle or a small victory within the family can ripple outward, advancing God's redemptive plan for a community, a nation, and ultimately, the world.

Reflect on the Chapter

* What was Hannah's plight, and how did she respond? What do you observe about Hannah's prayer?
* Which aspects of Hannah's story echo familiar themes of the larger Old Testament narrative?
* What is significant about Hannah's Song?

Reflect on Your Life

* Hannah was taunted by her rival and suffered social stigma because she did not have children. So Hannah poured out her heart to God in prayer. After praying and receiving a blessing from Eli, she was no longer sorrowful even though her situation had not yet changed. Have you ever experienced God lifting your spirits or lightening your burden after you prayed to him? If so, reflect on what that was like.
* Hannah dedicated her son Samuel to God by sending him to serve in the temple all the days of his life. What gift or blessing in your life are you tempted to hold on to for yourself that God may want you to surrender to him or share with others?
* Describe a time when you experienced God giving you strength beyond your own to face a difficult task.

Take Your Bold Step

* Hannah poured out her heart to God in lament over her infertility. She did not hold back her grief as she pleaded for God to give her a son. We sometimes are afraid of asking

God for specific desires of our hearts perhaps because we don't trust him or we don't want to be disappointed if he doesn't grant our plea. Take some time to pray a prayer of lament or a prayer expressing your heart's desire to God.

* Eli mistakenly assumed that Hannah was drunk when she was praying. But when he was corrected, Eli blessed Hannah and later taught Samuel how to listen to God's voice. Sometimes we make wrong assumptions about people because we don't know their stories. Take some time to ask curious questions and listen to someone's story. What is their background? What things do they care about? Notice how simply by listening and learning more about them, you allow God to open your heart to the person.

Breath Prayer

(Inhale)   Lord, my strength,
(Exhale)   help me to rise up.

CHAPTER 11

Recovering Bathsheba's Dignity

2 SAMUEL 11–12 AND 1 KINGS 1–2

The books of Samuel begin with Hannah, whose story weaves together key threads in the biblical narrative and whose son, Samuel, anoints Saul and then David as the first kings of Israel. As Hannah births a king-maker at the beginning of 1 Samuel, so Bathsheba births a king and participates with Nathan the prophet to ensure his ascent to the throne at the beginning of 1 Kings. But there's more, much more, to Bathsheba's story.

Bathsheba is a controversial and misunderstood figure. Many find it necessary to vilify her to protect their heroic image of David; therefore, Bathsheba may be the most wrongfully denigrated and sexualized woman in Scripture.[1] "At her best, she is read as a weak woman who is unable to stand up to the king's advances; at her worst, and perhaps more commonly, she is depicted as a seductress: a loose, immoral adulteress who schemed her way into the king's bed."[2]

However, rabbis view her as "a righteous, guiltless woman," for God never reprimands or punishes her. "The midrash [rabbinic interpretations and commentary on Scripture] asserts that the affair of David and Bathsheba was a trial that David brought upon himself, and which he failed."[3]

Any interpretation that places the blame on Bathsheba for David's actions cannot be found in the biblical evidence.

Bathsheba Within Samuel and Kings

Bathsheba's story begins both the downward turn of David's monarchy in 2 Samuel 11–12 and the ascent of Solomon's in 1 Kings 1–2. On the surface, she is an accessory to their stories. Upon closer examination, she's the pivot point for both of their monarchies: passively for David's and purposefully for Solomon's.

We've noted that in Scripture, men's treatment of women mirrors their spiritual condition, which reverberates into their family and often the nation. David, the "man after [God's] own heart" (1 Sam 13:14), is a leading figure in salvation history, but his undeterred lust for Uriah's wife sparks the fire that leads to murder and the division of the monarchy. When David "takes" Bathsheba and kills her husband, Uriah, in an attempted cover-up, he betrays his people and his covenant responsibilities.[4]

Cheryl You observes, "The David and Bathsheba narrative marks a major turning point in David's kingship. . . . [it] reminds us that the historian is not interested in whitewashing David, but in communicating that how kings act in relation to covenantal law have wide-ranging implications on the larger community of Israel."[5]

The narrative is framed by Bathsheba's name, which means "daughter of an oath." In the first half of her story, she is a daughter, a little ewe lamb, and a silent wife. However, the word "oath" returns in 1 Kings 1 as Bathsheba, through an oath, steps into a new role as queen mother and helps orchestrate Solomon's rise to kingship.

Investigating the Crime (2 Samuel 11)

After David's tremendous ascent from shepherd boy to king, gaining fame with the people and acclaim with God, in 2 Samuel 11 we enter a crime scene.

As with any good investigation, we examine the available data from the scene. David's role as king was to lead his army into battle for protection and conquest (see 1 Sam 8:5, 19–20), but instead he stayed home and sent his general Joab with the Israelite army. While neglecting his military duty, "one evening David got up from his bed and walked around on the roof of the palace. From the roof he saw a woman bathing. The woman was very beautiful" (2 Sam 11:2).

BATHSHEBA'S LUXURIOUS BATH?
THINK AGAIN (2 SAMUEL 11:2)

A common mistake is to read into this verse that Bathsheba is displaying herself. "Despite the fact that David saw Bathsheba 'from upon the roof' . . . it is not uncommon for biblical scholars to erroneously assume that Bathsheba is also standing on a rooftop while bathing,"[6] leading some to cast Bathsheba as a seductress.[7] For example, George G. Nicol argues that Bathsheba by "bathing in such close proximity to the royal palace was deliberately provocative."[8] Similarly, Randall Bailey calls Bathsheba a "willing and equal partner" with strong political aspirations of becoming David's wife and therefore sought to seduce him.[9]

First, a closer look at the text shows that the text gives David's location, not hers.[10] David is walking around his roof, which is high enough for "him to see through a window a woman bathing either in her own home or in the unroofed inner court of a typical four-room Israelite building."[11]

Archaeological data indicates that during the Iron Age (the time of David), washing in the home typically took place in an enclosed courtyard, not on roofs.[12] Unlike Renaissance paintings, modern movies, or sagas told about David and Bathsheba, there is no archaeological evidence of ancient Israelite families having luxurious stone or ceramic bathtubs hoisted on their roofs, with servants carrying clay or stone jugs filled with hot water to fill them for a lady's leisure.[13]

Second, nearly every English Bible translates 2 Samuel 11:2 as David saw a woman "bathing" *rkhts* (root pronounced *rakhatz*). Although that's not an overtly wrong translation, it is misleading. The same verb occurs in 2 Samuel 12:20 in reference to David, consistently translated "washed" himself after Bathsheba's baby died.* But in this context, the general translation of this verb, which is to "douse with water, wash off, wash," is a better translation.[14]

The images of Bathsheba bathing on top of the roof are, perhaps, male fantasies designed to stir imaginations and to justify King David as "a man's man" seduced by a longing temptress who is "asking for it."[15]

But there is no suggestion of nudity or seduction in the text. Her simple act of washing is "interrupted by the voyeuristic gaze of David" who sees her "as an object—a beautiful woman who is bathing."[16] Rather than taking his place as the king to lead battles, he dallies at home and seeks out another kind of conquest.[17]

WHO IS THE WOMAN?

Straightaway upon spotting the woman who catches his eye, "David sent and inquired regarding the woman, and he was told,

---

* The same verb *rkhts* in 2 Sam 11:2 used for Bathsheba occurs in 2 Sam 12:20 in the same stem (*qal*) used of David. The Septuagint also uses the same verb in the Greek, *louō*, in both passages to translate the Hebrew verb rkhts for washing, cleansing with water. After Bathsheba's first son died, David got up and "washed" (*rkhts*), put on lotion, and changed clothes. Nearly every English Bible translates this verse as David "washed" and not "bathed" even though it's the same verb in the same stem as for Bathsheba. However, the change in English verbs makes the visual imagery in each scene quite different. "Washed" is a better translation for Bathsheba's as well as David's action.

'Isn't this Bathsheba, the daughter of Eliam, the wife of Uriah the Hittite?'" (2 Sam 11:3, my translation).

Not only is she married, but her husband, Uriah, is one of David's warriors (2 Sam 23:39). If that's not enough, Bathsheba is the daughter of Eliam, another one of David's mighty men (2 Sam 23:34).* Moreover, her father, Eliam, is the son of Ahithophel, David's counselor. Bathsheba's grandfather is part of David's innermost circle of trusted advisors (2 Sam 15:12; 23:34; 1 Chr 27:33).[18]

David's disregard of God's law not to covet another man's wife and his betrayal of those who trusted him bring consequences into his life personally and upon the nation since he is their king.[19] It is hubristic for David to think that power or position could protect him from God's justice. There is no such thing as hidden sin.

Is It Rape? (2 Samuel 11:1–4)

After hearing her identity, David takes immediate action as if on a military quest, without conscience. "David sent messengers and he took her, and she came to him, and he lay with her (now she had been consecrating herself of her uncleanness), and she returned to her house" (2 Sam 11:4, my translation).

What does the verb "took" mean? Is this rape? As explained by Sandie Gravett, "Biblical Hebrew has no direct word for 'rape.'[20] Since there is 'no one-to-one correspondence between Hebrew and English' for 'sexual violence or violation,' an assessment of non-consensual sexual intercourse must be determined from the Hebrew within the context of the story."[21] So let's look at this passage closely to investigate the context of this scene.

---

* There is some debate if Eliam in 2 Samuel 23:34 is the same Eliam as in 2 Samuel 11:3, where he's named as Bathsheba's father. Eliam is also called Ammiel in 1 Chronicles 3:5, son of Ahithophel.

David Sends, Again and Again

In verse 3, after King David "sends" someone to find out who Bathsheba is, he disregards all the red flags warning "stay away!" Without a flicker of hesitation after hearing Bathsheba's identity and lineage, David sends messengers (plural) to her home, he (David) takes her, she comes to him, and he lays with her (euphemism for "has sex"). Then she returns to her house. Interjected in this swift sequence, just before she returns to her house, a parenthetical statement tells us that she was consecrating herself from her uncleanness (2 Sam 11:4).

The "rapid succession of verbs" in verses 3–4 indicates "overwhelming initiative on the part of David ('he saw . . . sent . . . inquired . . . sent . . . took her . . . lay with her . . .')." These actions by David are interrupted only by "she came to him."[22] The Hebrew verb for "to send" is used eleven times in this chapter, the most of any chapter in the Hebrew Bible, pointing to David's haste and "misuse of authority."[23]

To Take

The words from the Hebrew, David "saw" (*ra'ah*) that the woman "was good" (*tov*) in form and "took" (*laqakh*) her (2 Sam 11:2, 4, my translation), have a dark history in the Bible. Remember, the sequence of the words "saw" (*ra'ah*), "good" (*tov*), and "took" (*laqakh*) is connected with rebellion against God by taking for oneself what looks good but is forbidden by God (e.g., Gen 3:6; 6:1).[24]

The Hebrew word for "take" (*laqakh*) without adding "wife" when combined with "lie down" is associated with illicit sexual acts and rape. For instance, from the Hebrew in Genesis 6:2, the sons of Elohim "saw," (*ra'ah*) that the daughters of humans were "good" (*tov*) and "took" (*laqakh*) them, and "went into" (*bw'*) them. Shechem "saw" (*ra'ah*) and took (*laqakh*) Dinah and lay (*shkb*) with her (Gen 34:2).

In the Hebrew Bible the typical way to say that a man took a wife in marriage is by using two words together to "take a wife" (*laqakh ishah*). But to take a woman without using the word *ishah* (wife/woman) is considered "a base act."[25]

For consensual sex, whether in marriage or outside of marriage, the Hebrew Bible uses the words "to go into/enter her" and "to lay/lie with her" together, but if one of those words is not present or if the words are used without "wife," the sex is not consensual.[26] For example, after David marries Bathsheba and has sex with her again, the Hebrew uses the language of sex associated with marriage, which is translated as he "went in to her and lay with her" and includes the term "his wife" (2 Sam 12:24 NASB1995).

The emphatic repetition of "take" in 2 Samuel 11 also serves as a reminder of what Samuel had warned the elders of Israel of when they demanded a king: "It is here that the warnings of Samuel in 1 Sam. 8:11–18 come reverberating back through time: 'he will take your sons . . . he will take your daughters . . .' The phrase 'he will take' occurs six times, anticipating the king's abuse of power and authority, subjecting those under his rule to his whims and fancies."[27]

As Elna Solvang observes, "The theme underlying this story is not sex . . . but the royal power to 'take.'"[28]

SHE COMES TO HIM

Some scholars take the phrase that Bathsheba "came to him" as infused with sexual undertones or collusion. But they're missing the fact that David also *sends* for Uriah, who *comes to him* (2 Sam 11:6–7). Coming to the king is an act of compliance, not collaboration. "No choice is given, so the phrase cannot denote complicity, much less any semblance of consent."[29] Later, Yahweh *sends* Nathan to David, and Nathan *comes to him* (David) (2 Sam 12:1). For Nathan, coming to the king is an act of obedience to

Yahweh. Given these contexts, it's absurd to interject sexual implications.*

And notice David's decision to send more than one messenger to Bathsheba, whose husband is away at war, fighting for the king. David does not send an invitation by one messenger for her to be accompanied to the palace. David's sending of multiple messengers is a show of power. Bathsheba has no choice but to come to him.

To Consecrate or Purify

Curiously, within verse 4 *a circumstantial clause*, an added piece of information is interjected: "when she had purified herself from her uncleanness" (NASB1995). Let's look at the whole sentence: "David sent messengers and took her, and when she came to him, he lay with her; and when she had purified herself from her uncleanness, she returned to her house" (2 Sam 11:4 NASB1995).

This phrase has been interpreted two ways. The question is, What is the relationship and the timing between David taking and laying with Bathsheba and her consecrating herself?[30] Her act of consecration either refers back to her washing in verse 2 or reflects what she did during or after David took her for sex.

In support of the first view, the narrator may be taking the extra step in verse 4 to clarify that Bathsheba had been ritually cleansing herself after her menstrual cycle in verse 2. In this argument, David had sex with her while she was in the state of being ritually clean from her menstrual cycle (Lev 16:19–25). This would establish that she could not have conceived before Uriah left for battle.

However, this argument fails on account of the fact that the word for "to wash" (*rkhts*) is used seventy-seven times in the

---

* The phrase "she came to him" is a textual variant in the MT. It is missing in the Septuagint and in the Syriac Peshitta. Either the phrase is not original to the text, or "it could have been omitted to emphasize that it was not consensual." See Andruska, "'Rape' in the Syntax of 2 Samuel 11:4," 104, 107. See also Donald M. Walter et al., The Syriac Peshitta Bible with English Translation: Samuel (Piscataway, NJ: Gorgias, 2015), 260 f.

Hebrew Bible, but it "is never associated with a woman bathing following her menstrual period."[31] A woman is never told to wash because of her menstruation.[32] Also, the verb in verse 4 for consecrating (purifying) herself is absent from the laws of purification.

Furthermore, according to Hebrew grammar, the interjection about her consecrating herself "must be contemporaneous with the principal action of the preceding verb."[33] In other words, Bathsheba's act of consecrating herself from her uncleanness must be associated with the immediately preceding act in the sentence: David taking her for sex.

Therefore, the first option must be eliminated.

In support of the second view, the verb in verse 4, *qadash*, in general means "holy, removed from common use, subject to special treatment."[34] The particular form of this verb used in verse 4 (*mitqaddeshet* from *qadash*) occurs twenty-four times in the Hebrew Bible.* This is translated into English almost every time as "consecrate," *except* in 2 Samuel 11:4, where it is usually translated as Bathsheba "purifying herself."

A team of Hebrew scholars collaborated on an in-depth investigation of the use of "consecrate" (*mitqaddeshet*) and found that its use in verse 4 is unique. In all other places in the Hebrew Bible, it is used to refer to a group of people, priests, or Levites setting themselves apart for a particular service or purpose. "Bathsheba is the only individual human to sanctify herself of her own volition" in the Old Testament.[35] The following is their conclusion:

A smooth translation is difficult, but in order to keep the meaning of the phrase in the context of the Hebrew grammar, it must read:

---

* The stem of the verb used in 2 Sam 11:4 is known as the *hithpael* form of the verb *qadaš*. This form of the verb is always almost always translated into English as "consecrate" and occurs, for example, in Exod 19:22; Lev 20:7; Josh 7:13: 1 Sam 16:5; Isa 66:17; 1 Chr 15:12, 14; 2 Chr 29:15, 34; 30:3, 15, 17, 24.

David lay with her while simultaneously she is in a state of self-sanctifying. (2 Sam. 11.4)

It is unclear what the uncleanness is. The uncleanness cannot be menstruation; it must relate to David's action, which could include everything from unwanted sexual activity to the emission that results from the sexual activity (Lev. 15.16–18).[36]

The main point is that Bathsheba is presented as a woman of character who seeks to adhere to what is righteous before Yahweh and even exceed the requirements of Torah, consecrating herself even while being defiled.

The Verdict

The weight of the evidence makes the verdict clear: David raped Bathsheba, even if it was not violent. Bathsheba is portrayed as an object to be commanded and used, without voice, character, or autonomy. Brent Nessler likewise concludes, "The question of what exactly David has done to Bathsheba in the biblical narrative remains for many scholars an open question. To be sure, by modern medical and psychological standards, Bathsheba was raped by David, based, if for no other reason, on the massive power differential between a king and a vulnerable woman residing in a patriarchal society. The option to decline David's advance, and thus maintain any degree of agency, is not afforded to Bathsheba. Therefore, David raped Bathsheba."[37]

Second Samuel 11 closes with the words "But the thing which David had done was evil in the eyes of Yahweh" (v. 27 LEB). The verdict and consequent justice that God renders in this case confirms David's guilty charge, the weight of which his entire family and the nation must bear.

"I Am Pregnant" (2 Samuel 11:5)

We hear only two words (in the Hebrew) from Bathsheba in this narrative, sent as a message to the king. She gives only the facts: "The woman conceived and sent word to David, saying, 'I am pregnant'" (2 Sam 11:5). Her emotions and thoughts are withheld. But by sending the message to David, she calls him to account for his actions.

David does not respond to her.

Rather, "David does everything he should not do: he tries to cover up his sin by attempting to put the responsibility of paternity on his trusted warrior Uriah, and when that fails, he arranges to have Uriah killed" in battle.[38]

David's songs and prayers to God are entirely absent in this chapter. David is acting on impulse alone, without God or human council.

Bathsheba's Lament (2 Samuel 11:26–27)

"When the wife of Uriah heard that Uriah her husband was dead, she made lamentation for him. When the mourning was over, David sent and brought her to his house, and she became his wife and bore him a son" (2 Sam 11:26–27 NRSVue).

The only expression of Bathsheba's inner life we are privy to is here. When she hears of the death of her husband, she grieves. Elna Solvang writes that Bathsheba's mourning "draws attention to her position as victim of David's sending for her and of his sending Uriah to his death. . . . Like the lament of Rizpah in a subsequent chapter (2 Sam. 21:10–14), Bathsheba's lament functions as a judgment against royal violence directed at women and their families. Like Rizpah's lament it is followed by divine intervention."[39]

With still no sign of dialogue between David and Bathsheba,

he once again "sends" for her and gathers her to his house, and she becomes his wife and bears him a son.

This scene closes with the omniscient narrator giving God's assessment of everything David did in the preceding narrative: "But the thing that David had done was evil in the sight of the LORD" (2 Sam 11:27c NASB1995).

The next voice we hear is Nathan the prophet, who God now "sends" for David to call him to account for his evil.

When David and Bathsheba's son falls ill, we hear David mourning and praying, but we don't hear Bathsheba's lament. We are left only to imagine her grief upon grief from the multiplied trauma she experiences as a young woman. Thrust on her also is having to live in David's dysfunctional royal household as a young widow, a grieving mother, and an additional wife of the king.

After the death of the child, "then David comforted his wife Bathsheba, and he went to her and made love to her. She gave birth to a son, and they named him Solomon. The LORD loved him; and because the LORD loved him, he sent word through Nathan the prophet to name him Jedidiah" (2 Sam 12:24–25).

We don't know if Bathsheba was actually comforted by sex with David (I find it doubtful). And we don't hear her voice or her name again until David is nearing his death in 1 Kings 1.

Bathsheba the Mother

Bathsheba has four sons: Shammua (Shimea), Shobab, Nathan, and Solomon (2 Sam 5:14; 1 Chr 3:5). The first two are not mentioned elsewhere. Some suppose Nathan to be the son who died.[40] However, Nathan the son of David is listed in the genealogy of Joseph in Luke 3:31. In other words, of Bathsheba's four sons, we know only the story of Solomon. Nevertheless, we note that Bathsheba names one of her sons after the prophet who twice comes to defend her and who is in the genealogy of Mary's husband Joseph in the New Testament.

After Solomon is born, Yahweh himself takes special note of him and sends word through Nathan to call him Jedidiah (*yedideyah*), meaning "beloved of Yahweh" (2 Sam 12:25). Yahweh is "pointing to God's redemptive purposes in the midst of human sin and brokenness. Bathsheba is the victim of the king, the mighty one who has asserted his authority over her in a wrongful way. Jedidiah, the 'beloved of the Lord,' reminds the reader that God reverses the fortunes of the weak and elevates them."[41]

This scene is the last time we hear about Bathsheba or Nathan the prophet until David is approaching death and Solomon is a young man. Yet it foreshadows the future collaboration of Bathsheba and the prophet on behalf of the "beloved of Yahweh."

Meanwhile, from here until David's death, his family becomes a battlefield, which some years later implodes the nation into civil war. As Nathan prophesies, the sword does not leave David's household and eventually splits the kingdom in two. But not until after the reign of Solomon.

Bathsheba Speaks, and History Changes Course (1 Kings 1–2)

The book of 1 Kings opens with David as an old man, absent of his virility and unable to keep warm. David's servants find for him an exceptionally beautiful young virgin named Abishag to serve as his administrator (*sokheneth*)[42] and to keep him warm. But the narrative is careful to inform us that David did not "know" her, meaning he did not have sex with her (1 Kgs 1:2–4).

In David's declined state, his fourth and oldest living son, Adonijah, makes a play for the throne. David, as an emotionally and behaviorally absentee father never asks his son, "Why did you do that?" (1 Kgs 1:6, my translation). Adonijah recruits Joab the general and Abiathar the priest to support him and invites all his brothers to his coronation, except Solomon (1 Kgs 1:9–10).

The prophet Nathan returns to the scene for the first time since the birth of Solomon, this time to protect Solomon from David's negligence. Nathan and Bathsheba know that unless David names Solomon to the throne, he will most likely be killed because his existence is a threat to Adonijah's monarchy.[43]

Nathan reaches out to Bathsheba as the "mother of Solomon," not as David's wife. Prophet and mother join forces to strategically confront David in a crafted sequence of events so that he will declare Solomon as his successor. Nathan tells Bathsheba his strategy. She agrees, but contrary to Nathan's proposed strategy, she doesn't ask David questions. Instead, Bathsheba uses her own words, which are more effective, and "made pronouncements that stirred David to act kingly."[44] Bathsheba approaches David as a subject of the king and, more importantly, as the mother of the future king, determined to move King David to action. She relies on knowing the importance of his persona as king and speaks of his reputation.[45]

"She said to him, 'My lord, you yourself swore [*sheba*] to me your servant by the LORD your God: "Solomon your son shall be king after me, and he will sit on my throne." But now Adonijah has become king, and you, my lord the king, do not know about it'" (1 Kgs 1:17–18). Crucial to her tactic, Bathsheba begins with declaring the oath David swore to her. There's no such statement or evidence in the text of David making such an oath, except perhaps as a foreshadowing in Solomon's birth narrative being named "beloved of Yahweh" (2 Sam 12:24–25 NLT 2004).

She informs him of Adonijah's official enthronement ceremony currently taking place, appealing to his pride that he as king doesn't seem to know what's happening right under his nose. Then she calls out the king in him to rise to action: "My lord the king, the eyes of all Israel are on you, to learn from you who will sit on the throne of my lord the king after him. Otherwise, as soon as my lord the king is laid to rest with his ancestors, I and my son Solomon will be treated as criminals [i.e., killed or banished]" (1 Kgs 1:20–21).

Nathan—preceded by the pronouncement "Nathan the prophet is here"—then appears on cue (v. 22). He bows before the king (a reminder to David of who he still is) and confirms that Adonijah is being declared king as he speaks. He reinforces and reiterates what Bathsheba said and adds, "Is this something my lord the king has done without letting his servants know who should sit on the throne of my lord the king after him?" (1 Kgs 1:27).

Their strategy works. David swears an oath (*shb'*, or "sheba") to Bathsheba, saying, "As surely as the LORD lives, who has delivered me out of every trouble, I will surely carry out this very day what I swore [*sheba'*] to you by the LORD, the God of Israel: Solomon your son shall be king after me, and he will sit on my throne in my place" (1 Kgs 1:29–30).

In this narrative, the fullness of Bathsheba's name comes full circle. By declaring that David swore an oath to her and with David confirming this oath, she moves from being Bathsheba "daughter of an oath" to the mother of an oath, securing the throne for her son and ensuring her place as a queen mother.

David immediately steps into kingly action and calls for "a trio of kingmakers: priestly (Zadok), prophetic (Nathan), and military (Benaiah) leaders. These are the very men Nathan had told him were not invited to Adonijah's recent feast, and all whom would have been counted as offenders if David had chosen to support Adonijah's claim to the throne."[46]

Solomon is then saddled on a mule, taken to the Gihon Spring in Jerusalem (the official place of royal decrees), anointed with oil with trumpets blowing, and announced as king with the people rejoicing in the city (1 Kgs 1:36–40).

Enthronement and Resolution
of Bathsheba's story

After David gives Solomon parting advice and charges him to follow the laws of Moses, David dies, and Solomon is firmly established on the throne (1 Kgs 2:1–12). With Solomon on the throne of the kingdom, Adonijah and those who pledged their allegiance to him fear for their lives (1 Kgs 1:49–53).

The newly deposed Adonijah approaches Bathsheba to make a request on his behalf to King Solomon. She first inquires if he has come peacefully. He affirms, "Yes, peacefully," but immediately continues, "As you know . . . the kingdom was mine. All Israel looked to me as their king. But things changed" (1 Kgs 2:13–15). Then he asks her to request that Solomon give him Abishag as his wife. She agrees to speak to Solomon, understanding that "one of the customs of the ancient world was for the new king to confirm his position by taking the wives of the former king (2 Sam 16:22)" and that "Adonijah must have viewed Solomon as very weak to make this dangerous request."[47]

Evidence for Bathsheba's personal and political honor at this point is demonstrated as she approaches Solomon: "The king stood up to meet her, bowed down to her and sat down on his throne. He had a throne brought for the king's mother, and she sat down at his right hand" (1 Kgs 2:19).

Bathsheba shows that she has become a skilled strategist. When presenting Adonijah's appeal to Solomon, she adds the word "small": "I have one *small* request to make of you" (v. 20, emphasis added). She knows, as does Solomon, that taking Abishag is no "small request" but is understood as a power grab.[48] Gary Inrig affirms: "In the culture of the time, possession of the former king's harem was linked to a claim on the throne (see 2 Sam. 3:8; 16:20–22). Adonijah clung to the idea that he was the rightful king (**All Israel looked to me as their king**), and almost certainly this was the opening move for another attempt to displace Solomon."[49]

Thus, Bathsheba's words subtly emphasize Adonijah's audacity. Solomon has him put to death that day.

Brent Nessler observes well that "it is in 1 Kgs 2, then, that Bathsheba's story in the biblical text reaches an appropriate resolution. King David rapes her, and the prospective King Adonijah (implicitly) threatens to kill her, but King Solomon 'bows' (וחתשׁי) to her and provides a 'throne' (אסכ) at his right hand (v. 19)."[50] Rather than the portrayal of a flat character, "Bathsheba's story is a coherent narrative of resilient metamorphosis, from silenced victim to archetype of a voice reclaimed."[51]

Legacy of Bathsheba

Bathsheba stands at two key junctions in Scripture: at the descent of the reign of David and at the ascent to the throne of King Solomon just before David's death. As Cheryl You states, "Bathsheba is a difficult character to wrestle with, because, unlike Hannah and Abigail, her dialogue and actions are sparse within the text. The historian, however, does not view her as unimportant. She transitions from being a victim and symbol of David's abuse of kingly power into a woman of influence who ensures that Solomon, the 'beloved of the Lord,' continues David's legacy and God's plan for the monarchy."[52]

Bathsheba provides us with an example of a traumatized young woman who in rather rapid succession is raped, experiences the death of her husband and son, is torn from her home, and is forcibly married to her rapist. She starts out silent but finds her voice, saves her son Solomon, and reclaims their lives.

When it comes to evaluating trauma narratives in Scripture, one of the lenses through which the reader can assess recovery is whether the victim is shown in some capacity to overcome their ordeal. Healing of trauma is generally demonstrated through the recovery of their voice and agency, compared with the victim who remains silent, silenced, or shut out.[53]

Close study from the original language indicates that while David was desecrating Bathsheba, she was consecrating herself to Yahweh (2 Sam 11:4). She is the only person in the Old Testament to individually dedicate herself to God.[54] Studies of post-traumatic stress disorder have shown that a key factor that traps people in their trauma is "moral injury," the awareness of the violation done to their conscience as well as their body.[55] Her self-sanctification while being violated may point to a path forward at the critical moment of her deepest pain, helping her heal, recover her dignity, and regain her voice.

It's important to note the role of the prophet Nathan in Bathsheba's trauma. He speaks up when everyone else is silent, declaring God's justice and judgment. He is willing to stand up to the king and point the finger of God in his face, exposing the evils David tried to hide. Later, when the lives of Solomon and Bathsheba are at risk, Nathan invites Bathsheba's active participation in reversing Adonijah's usurpation of power and facilitates her opportunity to speak to David and reclaim a future for her and her son.

Robert Alter notes, "Whereas the beautiful young wife was accorded no dialogue except for her report to David of her pregnancy, the mature Bathsheba will show herself a mistress of language—shrewd, energetic, politically astute."[56] Bathsheba transforms from an object to be used to a "mother leader."[57] Although we're not privy to the years of Bathsheba's informal training in the affairs of state, her skill and wisdom are apparent as she masterfully influences the decisions of the elderly King David and her newly coronated son, King Solomon.

With her final scene, Bathsheba doesn't disappear into obscurity, but uses a gift that God gave uniquely to humans: she speaks and does so skillfully. Out of her trauma, she is able to declare a destiny for herself and Solomon, which progresses biblical history one step closer to the coming of the only perfect King.

Reflect on the Chapter

* Why do you think Bathsheba is a controversial, misunderstood, and even vilified character?
* What was your impression of Bathsheba before reading this chapter? How has your view of Bathsheba changed after reading this chapter?
* What adjectives would you use to describe Bathsheba in the beginning of the narrative (2 Sam 11–12)? What adjectives would you use to describe Bathsheba at the end of the narrative (1 Kgs 1–2)?

Reflect on Your Life

* Can you relate to the young Bathsheba, who is voiceless? If so, what has happened in your life that makes you feel silenced or voiceless?
* Or can you relate to the older Bathsheba, who uses her voice to influence the course of events? If so, what has helped you find your voice?
* What in your life needs healing? What are you doing or can you do to pursue healing and recovery?

Take Your Bold Step

* According to Dr. Faro, Bathsheba consecrated herself even while being defiled, demonstrating her righteous character. In what ways can you devote yourself to God even when the people around you aren't following him?

* Bathsheba appealed to David's sense of pride and reputation to stir him to act. Sometimes we must initiate hard conversations to effect positive change. Is there a conversation you need to have with someone to open their eyes or help them act for good? How would you approach that conversation?

Breath Prayer

(Inhale)   God, my strength,

(Exhale)   help me speak your words.

CHAPTER 12

Jehosheba Saves the Line of David

2 KINGS 11

Few have ever heard of Jehosheba. Her story is short but not to be missed! About 135 years after King David dies, the patrilineal line of David is just a sword's slash away from annihilation. Without Jehosheba's brave and quick action, there would be no genealogy in Matthew or Luke.

The prophet Nathan told King David that when he despised God by taking the life and the wife of his trusted warrior Uriah, his lineage would be divided by strife and murder. We enter this story about five generations later, when both the nation and the monarchy have been marred by civil wars and idolatry.

The Background of Jehosheba's Story

After Solomon dies, his son Rehoboam becomes king. He foolishly listens to terrible advice, which divides the nation and leaves only two tribes loyal to him: Judah and Benjamin. These two tribes, along with the Levites, make up the southern kingdom of Judah. The other ten tribes become the northern kingdom of Israel under King Jeroboam I, a former servant of Solomon who rebelled against him. Every king of the breakaway northern kingdom of

Israel does evil in the eyes of God, worshiping Baal with the animal and human sacrifices that it requires. Time passes. Wars are fought between Israel and Judah and the surrounding nations.

In an effort to create stability between the southern kingdom of Judah and the northern kingdom of Israel, Rehoboam's great-great-grandson King Jehoshaphat of Judah forges a political alliance with King Ahab of Israel. The treaty includes the marriage of Jehoshaphat's son Jehoram to Athaliah, daughter of Ahab and perhaps Jezebel* (2 Kgs 8:18, 26).[1]

King Jehoram of Judah acts like "the true son of Ahab and Jezebel," embracing his wife Athaliah's worship of Baal.[2] To further secure his throne, Jehoram kills his six brothers and their sons, "who were better men than [him]" (2 Chr 21:13 GNT). In response, Elijah the prophet sends Jehoram a letter with the word of the Lord condemning his evil ways and abominations, saying, "So now the LORD is about to strike your people, your sons, your wives and everything that is yours, with a heavy blow. You yourself will be very ill with a lingering disease of the bowels, until the disease causes your bowels to come out" (2 Chr 21:14–15).

True to the prophet's word, neighboring marauding bands carry away Jehoram's sons and their families, except for his youngest son, Ahaziah. Jehoram's eight-year reign ends with the fulfillment of Elijah's prophecy: He dies in great pain with his bowels fallen out. The narrator concludes, "He passed away, to no one's regret, and was buried in the City of David, but not in the tombs of the kings" (2 Chr 21:20). Even though, Jehoram "did evil in the eyes of the LORD. [19] Nevertheless, for the sake of his servant David, the LORD was not willing to destroy Judah. He had promised to maintain a lamp for David and his descendants forever" (2 Kgs 8:17–18).

---

* The lineage of Athaliah is uncertain and debated. She may have been the daughter of Omri (2 Kgs 8:26; 2 Chr 22:2) and adopted by Ahab, or, the daughter of Ahab and Jezebel, or, stepdaughter of Jezebel (2 Kgs 8:18; 2 Chr 21:6). Regardless, Athaliah was clearly tutored by Jezebel as a faithful Baal worshiper and ruthless political leader 2 Kgs 11).

Jehoram's only remaining son, Ahaziah, is declared king at the age of twenty-two (2 Kgs 8:25–26). His mother, Athaliah, influences him to continue in the ways of Ahab, worshiping Baal. He reigns only one year and is killed while visiting his relative, the king of Israel.

Now both Jehoram and Ahaziah are dead. None of young Ahaziah's sons are old enough to assume the throne. Queen mother Athaliah has the sons of Ahaziah killed to take the throne and retain her power as ruler in Judah.[3] The line of David, the hope for the One to come, is wiped out . . . or so Athaliah thought. Gary Inrig rightly observes, "Humanly speaking, that line never came as close to extinction as it did at this moment in history. Because of Jehoram's purge of his brothers (2 Chr. 21:4), the killing of the royal family by Philistine and Arab raiders (2 Chr. 21:16–17), and the slaughter of her grandsons by Athaliah (2 Kgs. 11:1), only one male child of the Davidic royal line survived. The preservation of Joash was an event of great significance."[4]

And it was due to the swift, courageous actions of one woman.

Saving Baby Joash

Enter Jehosheba. Her name means "Yahweh is an oath." Jehosheba is a princess, daughter of Jehoram, sister of Ahaziah, and the wife of Jehoida the high priest (2 Chr 22:11; cf. 2 Chr 24:6–7).[5] Jehosheba is God's secret agent. God works through her. Although she grew up in the same household as her wicked brother Ahaziah and her evil father, Jehoram, and stepmother, Athaliah, she is faithful to Yahweh, as was her grandfather Jehoshaphat. And Jehosheba, married to the high priest Jehoiada, is faithful to Yahweh.

After the queen mother Athaliah begins killing all the "seed" (descendants) of the royal family, Jehosheba enters the palace and steals away the youngest and only surviving heir to the throne, Joash, son of King Ahaziah. She and Jehoiada hide him and his nurse in the bed chambers of the temple for six years, saving the line of David and the Messiah (2 Kgs 11:2–3; 2 Chr 22:11). Her "quick and sustained actions to preserve life made possible the coup six years later led by Jehoiada, the priest." [6]

She and her husband along with the rest of the priests bear the risk for six years of concealing the baby and his nurse in the temple. Jehoiada secures the cooperation of the priests and guards until the time is ripe to overthrow the worshipers of Baal and restore the kingdom to the Davidic line.

God always finds a way to fulfill his word and his promises. And God works through people to accomplish his plans.

Legacy of Jehosheba

We're told very little about Jehosheba, but without her brave actions, redemption history through the line of David would have been brought to an end by a Baal worshiper. The narrative of God's intervention is told through the story of human courage. Karen Winslow notes the connection to the exodus.

> Like the pharaoh of Exodus 1–2, Athaliah felt threatened by sons, allowing daughters to live, yet it was a daughter who saved a small son, just as daughters saved Moses—his sister, his mother, and Pharaoh's own daughter. . . . [7]
>
> As an infant, Joash escaped death at the hands of his grandmother because of the swift action of his aunt Jehosheba. We recall the similar fashion by which Moses escaped death at the hands of the king. . . . Clever women rescued future leaders for the sake of God's people.[8]

Jehosheba's name doesn't appear again. The genealogy in Matthew 1 lists her grandfather Jehoshaphat and her father Jehoram but skips over the next three kings, Ahaziah, Joash, and

Amaziah, and continues on with Uzziah the grandson of Joash (Matt 1:8). However, Jehosheba and her story are not overlooked by God in Scripture.

God works through human agency in ways we don't understand. He delights in stories of reversal, the subversion of worldly power and ambition through the overlooked or underestimated. The line of David hung by a thread, but God's promises are stronger.

When chaos and death strike, God prompts the hearts of those who hear him not to be paralyzed by evil but to look for opportunities to right the wrongs around us by moving into action and taking the next right step—to stop an injustice, to save a life, to protect the vulnerable.

Reflect on the Chapter

- What led to the division of Solomon's kingdom?
- What events put the line of David at risk before Jehosheba entered the story?
- How did God work through Jehosheba to preserve the Davidic line?

Reflect on Your Life

- Jehosheba followed in the spiritual footsteps of her grandfather Jehoshaphat. Think of the generations that came before you in your family: What kind of spiritual legacy did they leave for you to follow? In what ways do you want to emulate them, and in what ways do you want to avoid the path they chose?
- Jehosheba, her husband the high priest, and the rest of the priests worked together to hide Joash in the temple. They needed to trust one another to keep the secret to protect

all of their lives. In our individualistic society, relying on others can be seen as weak. But trusting and depending on others can actually be an act of courage. In what ways can you grow in trusting others and work together toward a common goal?

Take Your Bold Step

❋ Jehosheba and the priests kept Joash hidden for six years. Do you know someone who is unrecognized or unseen for their courageous and faithful acts of service? Do something to show them that you appreciate their ongoing faithfulness.

Breath Prayer

(Inhale)   God of David,
(Exhale)   thank you for your faithfulness.

Women in the Gospels and Beyond

G od's strategic placement of women in Scripture continues from the Old Testament into the New. While the women in the Old Testament boldly advance the storyline of Scripture by preparing the way for the Messiah through their prophetic, faithful, and bold actions, the women in the New Testament witness and testify to the good news of the Messiah at key moments of Jesus's birth, death, and resurrection.

The prominent placement of women in the Gospels shows how God continues to uplift, honor, and work through women for his redemptive purposes. In the opening chapter of the gospel of Matthew, four brave women of the Old Testament are woven into Jesus's family lineage, connecting the Old and New Testaments by the genealogy of Jesus the Messiah. In Luke, the perspectives of three women center the birth narrative of Jesus. And in all four gospels, it is women at the cross who follow the body of Jesus to his tomb and who are the first of his followers to witness his resurrection and tell others the good news. Let's take note of these women.

Women in the Genealogy of Jesus (Matthew 1)

The first women we encounter in Matthew 1 are Tamar, Rahab, Ruth, and Bathsheba, who are listed in the genealogy of the

Messiah (Matt 1:5–6). Each of these women put their faith in Yahweh and acted courageously for the continuation of their family or family line, which ultimately led to the birth of the Messiah. The stories that these names recall from the Old Testament remind us that redemption history grows out of the root of the Old Testament, which was the Bible of Jesus and his disciples.

The gentile (non-Israelite) background of Tamar, Rahab, and Ruth is fertile ground for the good news God promises from the beginning of humanity. Through them, we see the ongoing story of God's outstretched grace. God's love for the world and all people in it is demonstrated through his long-planned coming of Jesus as the Messiah. Each of these women participates in making history, unaware that the threads of their faithfulness and fortitude are woven into God's uniquely magnificent plan.

Women in the Birth Narrative of Jesus (Luke 1–2)

Luke's account of the birth narrative of Jesus prominently features three women. Through each one we hear echoes of the stories of the women who went before them, inspiring their faith.

First, we meet Elizabeth, mother of John the Baptist and wife of Zechariah. Her story begins, "Both of them [Elizabeth and Zechariah] were righteous in the sight of God, observing all the Lord's commands and decrees blamelessly. But they were childless because Elizabeth was not able to conceive, and they were both very old" (Luke 1:6–7). This reminds us of the barren-wife narratives of Sarah, Rebekah, Rachel, and Hannah, where God orchestrates a miraculous event that erases their shame and carries forward his greater plan of redemption.

Elizabeth's name, *Elisheba* in the Hebrew, means "God is my oath." Her name, embedded with the language of "oath" (*sheba'*), recalls Bathsheba and Jehosheba, who each advanced redemptive history by preserving the line of David. The son whom Elizabeth conceives becomes John the Baptist: "And he will go on before the Lord, in the spirit and power of Elijah, to turn the hearts of the parents to their children and the disobedient to the wisdom of the righteous—to make ready a people prepared for the Lord" (Luke 1:17).

Many elements of Elizabeth's story are like Hannah's: the grief of barrenness; prayer for a son (at the tabernacle for Hannah, at the temple for Elizabeth's husband, Zechariah); and the dedication of their sons, Samuel and John, who are both consecrated before their birth to serve God (1 Sam 1; Luke 1:8–25). When Elizabeth is six months pregnant, the angel Gabriel appears to her relative, Mary, in Nazareth, and their stories intertwine.

Mary is betrothed to Joseph, of the line of David. The angel Gabriel greets Mary and tells her, "You will conceive and give birth to a son, and you are to call him Jesus. He will be great and will be called the Son of the Most High. The Lord God will give him the throne of his father David, and he will reign over Jacob's descendants forever; his kingdom will never end" (Luke 1:31–33). She asks how this can happen since she's a virgin. Gabriel informs her that her relative Elizabeth, "who was said to be unable to conceive" (v. 36), is pregnant. Impossible? No! Gabriel explains, "For no word from God will ever fail" (v. 37). This is often translated, "For nothing will be impossible with God" (NRSVue, NET, NASB, LEB). It could also be translated, "For no word [*rhema*] of God will be without power."

Gabriel's words to Mary nearly match those spoken to Sarah way back in Genesis 18, when Sarah hears that she will give birth to a son long past her ability to conceive. Yahweh said, "Is anything too difficult for the LORD?" (Gen 18:14 NASB, CEB). Interestingly, in the Septuagint (early Greek translation of the Hebrew Bible), these words spoken by Yahweh are nearly identical to the words spoken by Gabriel in Luke 1:37.

It is likely that Mary connects the news of Elizabeth's miraculous pregnancy with the words Gabriel speaks to her that were once spoken to Sarah: With God, nothing is impossible. Mary's faith is engaged, and she responds simply with, "I am the Lord's servant. . . . May your word to me be fulfilled" (Luke 1:38).

Mary then hurries to see Elizabeth, still in her sixth month of pregnancy.

> When Elizabeth heard Mary's greeting, the baby leaped
> in her womb, and Elizabeth was filled with the Holy Spirit. In
> a loud voice she exclaimed: "Blessed are you among women,
> and blessed is the child you will bear! But why am I so favored,
> that the mother of my Lord should come to me? As soon as the
> sound of your greeting reached my ears, the baby in my womb
> leaped for joy. Blessed is she who has believed that the Lord
> would fulfill his promises to her!" (Luke 1:41–45)

Mary's prophetic song immediately follows Elizabeth's inspired utterance (Luke 1:46–55). Mary's Song, "The Magnificat," bears a striking resemblance to Hannah's prophetic song in 1 Samuel 2.[1] As with Hannah's Song, "In Mary's song she blesses God and specifically highlights the theme of [Luke] 1:45, which will continue to find emphasis throughout Luke. In other words," Douglas Mangum continues, "God has reversed the roles commonly held in the world; he has exalted the poor, rejected, and oppressed, and he has humbled the rich, proud, and esteemed."[2] Mary's Song concludes with the prophetic words that through her son, God's promises to Abraham will be fulfilled, that through him all people of the earth will be blessed (Luke 1:54–55).

Jesus is born! In him, all the threads of the themes come together. Eve's ancient hope in the seed of the woman crushes the head of the serpent. Tamar's righteous insistence on justice brings forth the Lion of the tribe of Judah. The women of the exodus story who risk their lives to save Moses leads to Jesus delivering us out of our slavery to sin and darkness. Rahab, who saved the Israelite spies, is rescued along with her family by hanging a red cord from her window, imaging the blood of the Passover lamb, until Christ's blood rescues all who receive him. The kinsman-redeemer in Ruth is fulfilled in her family line by the ultimate Redeemer for all humankind.

I don't have the space here to speak of all the women in Scripture who refused to give in to despair or give up their hope and dignity, not realizing their courage was saving lives, rescuing cities, and preparing the way for Jesus. The Messiah comes through women who experienced barrenness, slavery, injustice, famine, rape, exile, and near extermination. Through their suffering, these women exhibited perseverance, resourcefulness, compassion, valor, and loyal love. They prayed over, nurtured, protected, dedicated, and raised children to be faithful to Yahweh. They confronted in-laws, spouses, elders, leaders, rulers, generals, and kings.

When the Messiah is born, his presence is known! When he is forty days old, Mary and Joseph take Jesus to the temple in Jerusalem to fulfill the requirements of the Torah. Simeon recognizes Jesus and declares that now he can die in peace because he has seen the Lord's Messiah. Moments later, Luke tells us, "There was also a prophet, Anna, the daughter of Penuel, of the tribe of Asher. She was very old; she had lived with her husband seven years after her marriage, and then was a widow until she was eighty-four. She never left the temple but worshiped night and day, fasting and praying. Coming up to them at that very moment, she gave thanks to God and spoke about the child to all who were looking forward to the redemption of Jerusalem" (Luke 2:36–38).

Anna is specifically called a prophet, continuing the legacy of Miriam, Deborah, and Huldah into the New Testament.[3] Her name in Hebrew is Hannah, hinting that as Samuel inaugurated the monarchy, this child, Jesus, is inaugurating a new kingdom. But this time, the child himself is the king who will overturn the expectations of the wealthy and powerful as well as the poor and needy. Anna's father's name, Penuel, means "the face of God" in Hebrew.[4] This is the same name that Jacob called the place where he wrestled with God when he "saw God face to face" (Gen 32:30 [Hebrew, 32:31; LXX 32:32]). And now Anna sees the Messiah face to face.

Anna, like Simeon, identifies Jesus as the long promised one to come! Once Simeon takes Jesus in his arms and praises the Lord, he is prepared to die. But Anna, "unlike Simeon, goes forth to proclaim the good news about the Messiah."[5] As Luke reports, she "spoke about the child to all who were looking forward to the redemption of Jerusalem" (Luke 2:38). With her heart filled with joy and gratitude, Anna, who spent most of her life as a widow in the temple, is the first to spread the gospel, which means "good news!"

Women at the Cross

Finally, women play a significant role in the Gospels at the cross, the tomb, and the resurrection of Jesus Christ. At the crucifixion of Jesus, of his eleven remaining disciples, only John is present. But each gospel writer gives a partial listing of the women who joined Mary, the mother of Jesus, at the cross.

Matthew records, "Many women were there, watching from a distance. They had followed Jesus from Galilee to care for his needs. Among them were Mary Magdalene, Mary the mother of James and Joseph,[6] and the mother of Zebedee's sons" (Matt 27:55–56). Mark gives the name of the mother of James and Joseph as Salome and notes that "many other women who had come up with him to Jerusalem were also there" (Mark 15:41).[7] During Jesus's ministry, many of these same women from Galilee had been following him from town to town and were helping to financially support Jesus and the disciples (Luke 8:2–3).

John focuses on those close enough to hear his last words: "Near the cross of Jesus stood his mother, his mother's sister, Mary the wife of Clopas, and Mary Magdalene. When Jesus saw his mother there, and the disciple whom he loved [John] standing nearby, he said to her, 'Woman, here is your son,'[27] and to the disciple, 'Here is your mother.' From that time on, this disciple took her into his home" (John 19:25–27). Jesus provided for his mother as one of his last acts on earth.

Women at the Tomb and the Resurrection of Christ

All four gospels report that the women were the first to discover the empty tomb, the first to witness Jesus's resurrection, and the first to share the good news with the apostles. They vary in mentioning which women were present. Matthew notes that Mary Magdalene and the other Mary went to look at the tomb (Matt 28:1). Mark gives a similar report, adding Salome (Mark 16:1). Luke speaks of more women going to the tomb—Mary Magdalene, Joanna, Mary the mother of James, and the others with them—who told the apostles and other men with them that Jesus is risen (Luke 24:1–12).

John focuses on the leading role of Mary Magdalene, who seems to be the first one to find the tomb empty. She arrives while it is still dark. After she sees that Jesus's body is gone, she runs to tell Peter and John. They run to the tomb, see, and believe. They still don't understand or remember Jesus's words to them foretelling his resurrection, and most return to their homes.

But Mary Magdalene returns to the tomb, weeping, and sees two angels inside who talk with her. John adds that when she turns away from the tomb, a man asks her, "'Woman, why are you crying? Who is it you are looking for?' Thinking he was the gardener, she said, 'Sir, if you have carried him away, tell me where you have put him, and I will get him.' Jesus said to her, 'Mary.' She turned toward him and cried out in Aramaic, 'Rabboni!' (which means 'Teacher')" (John 20:15–16).

John is not forgetting biblical symbolism when he mentions that Mary thinks the man before her is the gardener. Figuratively and in truth, Mary has returned to the garden of Eden: the Lord is risen, the curse is broken, death is defeated. Eden is redeemed and continues to be redeemed until Jesus returns to usher in the final redemption: the new heavens and the new earth.

Just as God places women at key junctures in Scripture, Jesus strategically chooses women as the first "apostles" to the apostles, sent to proclaim the good news of his resurrection.[*] In the first-century Jewish and Greco-Roman world, the testimony of women was considered unreliable and invalid in formal legal settings, yet women are the first to witness the empty tomb and to testify to the risen King![†] Defying cultural expectations, all four gospels highlight the vital role of women in bearing witness to Jesus's death, burial, and resurrection. Mary Magdalene's loyal love for the Lord in particular, "qualified her to be the first missionary with the full story."[8]

Considering how God casts women in these prominent and honorable roles in key moments of redemptive history throughout the Old and New Testament, it is undeniable that God values women and created them as image bearers and equal partners with men in his redemptive plan. Throughout Scripture, woman

---

[*]   William Arndt et al., *A Greek-English Lexicon of the New Testament and Other Early Christian Literature* (Chicago: University of Chicago Press, 2000), 120–22; Note that "apostle" is *apostolos* in Greek, meaning "messenger, envoy," which comes from the Greek verb *apostellō*, meaning "to dispatch someone for the achievement of some objective, send away/out" (italics original).

[†]   By the writing of the Talmud (between the third and sixth centuries AD), women were not considered valid witnesses.

after woman rises up as a strong ally (*ezer*), holding up her side (*tsela*) as a sacred image testifying to the glory of God.

The Legacy Continues

The New Testament and early church continue to speak of women proclaiming the good news of the Messiah, such as Mary and Martha of Bethany, the Samaritan woman at the well, Phoebe, Junia, Priscilla, Lydia, and many others.[9] Many more stories of courageous women faithfully serving God are present in Scripture and have proliferated in church history and around the world today. Women named and unnamed, known and unknown, are part of redemption history and part of redeeming Eden in the Bible and beyond. The stories continue through every woman who follows the Lord through joys and pains, successes and hardships, triumphs and traumas.

For God's kingdom to manifest here on earth, as it is in heaven, eyes must be open to see others and our own selves through God's eyes. In the world's system, heads turn to people of power and influence, prestige and popularity. But God gives heed to the humble who are doing justice and loving mercy. Courage is not the lack of fear but acting in the face of fear. So also, boldness is not a lack of humility but the determination to change what is wrong.

When we ignore those who may appear insignificant or different or make us uncomfortable, we fail to recognize what God is doing in our midst. Scripture reminds us that our thoughts are not God's thoughts, and our ways are not his ways (Isa 55:8).

Through Jesus, we witness the heart of God for women and all who are hurting or ignored. Jesus consistently showed respect to women, protected women and the defenseless, and dignified the women who followed him. Jesus's words and actions were and are countercultural to any power that seeks to elevate itself above others. Jesus said, "Anyone who has seen me has seen the Father" (John 14:9). Therefore, any opinion we have of God that doesn't look like Jesus is flawed.

As we've seen, God longs to fill our emptiness and redeem injustice. God seeks to overturn evil, bringing good out of painful circumstances and the harmful actions of others. But this requires our cooperation and persistence.

May we not underestimate what God can do in and through us, no matter the circumstances of our birth, no matter our social or cultural situation, no matter our age or position. God sees us, like he saw Hagar in the wilderness. He gives us strength to do spiritual battle, like Deborah. He hears and answers our heartfelt prayers, like he did for Hannah. Through our faith and love, God miraculously births new things in and through us. Our stories matter to God, and we are part of his greater story of redemption that he is still writing today. For the kingdom to advance on earth and Eden to be redeemed, women must continue to rise up to fulfill their God-given roles and callings as *ezers* and *tselas*, and men must welcome and serve alongside women. May we grow to believe in the capacity of ourselves and others to bring about God-inspired change when infused with his redemptive and loyal love.

Jesus the Messiah is coming again, for one church, one people of God composed of men and women from all nations and languages, working and serving together. Celebrating the gifts and differences that each one brings to the body of Christ, we manifest God's presence until Christ's return makes all things new and redeems Eden.

Reflect on the Chapter

* Where does God place women in key moments in the Gospels?

- Which women are chosen to be the first to witness and proclaim the good news?
- What traits do the women featured in this book have in common?

Reflect on Your Life

- Which woman from this book do you identify with most, and why?
- God continues to write his redemptive story in and through our stories. Many of the women in this book had no idea they were playing key roles in advancing salvation history and redeeming Eden. They were just following God boldly and faithfully. In what ways have you glimpsed God writing a redemptive story in your life?

Take Your Bold Step

- What kind of legacy would you like to leave in your family, in your work or ministry, or in your community?
- What step or change can you make now to move toward leaving that kind of legacy?

Breath Prayer

(Inhale)   I am your servant.
(Exhale)   Fulfill your word to me.

Notes

INTRODUCTION

1. Jacob L. Wright, *Why the Bible Began: An Alternative History of Scripture and Its Origins* (New York: Cambridge University Press, 2023), 357.
2. Todd L. Patterson, *The Plot-Structure of Genesis*, Lam ed., Biblical Interpretation Series 160 (Leiden: Brill, 2018), 212.
3. G. K. Beale, *God Dwells Among Us: Expanding Eden to the Ends of the Earth* (IVP, 2015).

CHAPTER 1: MAN AND WOMAN AS GOD'S IMAGE

1. *Hidden Figures*, directed by Theodore Melfi (20th Century Fox, 2016).
2. Catherine L. McDowell, *The Image of God in the Garden of Eden: The Creation of Humankind in Genesis 2:5–3:24 in Light of the Mīs Pî, Pīt Pî, and Wpt-r Rituals of Mesopotamia . . . and Theology of the Hebrew Scriptures)*, 1st ed. (Winona Lake, IN: Eisenbrauns, 2015), 1.
3. *The Koren Siddur* 1 ,נוסח ספרד: נוסח קורן סידורst Hebrew/English ed. (Jerusalem: Koren Publishers, 2012), xlv.
4. *Koren Siddur*, xxxvii.
5. Ludwig Koehler, Walter Baumgartner, and Johann Jakob Stamm, *The Hebrew and Aramaic Lexicon of the Old Testament*, trans. M. E. J. Richardson, CD-ROM (Leiden, Netherlands: Brill NV, 1994), 1219.
6. Ingrid Faro, *Demystifying Evil: A Biblical and Personal Exploration* (Downers Grove, IL: IVP Academic, 2023), 173–74.
7. W. Randall Garr, *In His Own Image and Likeness: Humanity, Divinity, and Monotheism* (Leiden: Brill Academic Pub, 2003), 201.
8. Carmen Joy Imes, *Being God's Image: Why Creation Still Matters* (Downers Grove, IL: IVP Academic, 2023), 27.

9. Jonathan Sacks, *Koren Shalem Siddur, Ashkenaz*, Bilingual ed. (Jerusalem: Koren Publishers Jerusalem, 2017), xxviii.

10. G. K. Beale, *The Temple and the Church's Mission: A Biblical Theology of the Dwelling Place of God* (Downers Grove, IL: IVP Academic, 2004). Richard Davidson, "Earth's First Sanctuary: Genesis 1–2 and Parallel Creation Accounts," *Andrews University Seminary Studies*, 2015; his footnote 65n.1 contains extensive references. Seung Il Kang, "The Garden of Eden as an Israelite Sacred Place," *Theology Today* (2020), 90.

11. Imes, *Being God's Image*, 24–27.

12. C. John Collins, *Genesis 1–4: A Linguistic, Literary, and Theological Commentary* (Phillipsburg, NJ: P & R Pub, 2006), 44.

13. Imes, *Being God's Image*, 16.

14. Imes, 4–6, convinced me to translate with the preposition "as" the image, with the meaning "serving as, in the capacity of," i.e., indicating that God made humans "to serve in the capacity intended for an image."

15. The Hebrew uses the singular pronominal suffix here, but in the Hebrew, the masculine singular can be inclusive or neutral.

16. The Hebrew uses the plural pronominal suffix here.

17. Imes, *Being God's Image*, 34–35. For further reading on the divine council, see Faro, *Demystifying Evil*, 191–93, 197–99; Michael S. Heiser, "Divine Council," in *The Lexham Bible Dictionary*, ed. John D. Barry et al. (Bellingham, WA, 2016).

18. McDowell, *The Image of God in the Garden of Eden*.

19. W. Randall Garr, "'Image' and 'Likeness' in the Inscription from Tell Fakharieh," *Israel Exploration Journal* 50, no. 3 (2000): 227–34.

20. McDowell, *The Image of God in the Garden of Eden*, 119.

21. Daniel E. Fleming, "Religion," in *Dictionary of the Old Testament: Pentateuch* (Downers Grove, IL: InterVarsity Press, 2002), 683.

CHAPTER 2: MAN AND WOMAN AS SACRED SPACE

1. John Goldingay, *Biblical Theology: The God of the Christian Scriptures* (Downers Grove, IL: IVP academic, an imprint of InterVarsity Press, 2016), 39; the modern fundamentalist church

culture's prioritization of a "maleness" to God has concealed his person and character, and obscured the fact that "The First Testament gives God more or less all body parts, but not genitals, though it does attribute to God breasts and a womb."

2. Catherine L. McDowell, *The Image of God in the Garden of Eden: The Creation of Humankind in Genesis 2:5–3:24 in Light of the Mīs Pî, Pīt Pî, and Wpt-r Rituals of Mesopotamia . . . and Theology of the Hebrew Scriptures)*, 1st ed. (Winona Lake, IN: Eisenbrauns, 2015), 138; and Gordon John Wenham, *Genesis 1–15*, ed. David Allen Hubbard, Glenn W. Barker, and John D. W. Watts, Word Biblical Commentary 1 (Grand Rapids: Zondervan Academic, 2014), 70. (The term "flesh and blood" traced through both Old Testament and New Testament refers to our humanity.)

3. Curt Thompson, *Anatomy of the Soul: Surprising Connections Between Neuroscience and Spiritual Practices That Can Transform Your Life and Relationships*, 3rd ed. (Carol Stream, IL: Tyndale, 2010), 137.

4. Jacqueline E. Lapsley, *Whispering the Word: Hearing Women's Stories in the Old Testament*, annotated ed. (Louisville, Ky: Westminster John Knox Press, 2005), 14.

5. "Command" in Gen 2:16 is from the verb *tswh*, "to give an order, command."

6. Lapsley, *Whispering the Word*, 15.

7. J. Baird Callicott, "Genesis and John Muir," in *Covenant for a New Creation: Ethics, Religion, and Public Policy*, ed. Carol S. Robb and Carl J. Casebolt (Maryknoll, NY: Orbis, 1991), 123 (italics original).

8. Karen Armstrong, *In the Beginning: A New Interpretation of Genesis* (New York: Knopf, 1996), 30.

9. "The biblical evidence for this conclusion has been documented by scores of biblical scholars"; Richard Davidson, "Earth's First Sanctuary: Genesis 1–2 and Parallel Creation Accounts," *Andrews University Seminary Studies*, 2015, 65; his footnote 65n.1 contains extensive references; see also L. Michael Morales, *Who Shall Ascend the Mountain of the Lord? A Biblical Theology of the Book of Leviticus* (Downers Grove, IL: IVP Academic, 2015), 93, 102.

10. Lifsa Block Schachter, "The Garden of Eden as God's First Sanctuary," *Jewish Bible Quarterly* (June 2013), 74.

11. G. K. Beale, *God Dwells Among Us: Expanding Eden to the Ends of the Earth* (IVP, 2015).

12. For a rich understanding of this, read J. Richard Middleton, *A New Heaven and a New Earth: Reclaiming Biblical Eschatology*, illustrated ed. (Grand Rapids: Baker Academic, 2014).

13. McDowell, *The Image of God in the Garden of Eden*, 157–58, 194. McDowell demonstrates the use of the verb *nwḥ* in the second hiphil in ritual practice of installation of a person or religious object. See also Ludwig Koehler, Walter Baumgartner, and Johann Jakob Stamm, *The Hebrew and Aramaic Lexicon of the Old Testament, 2 Volume Set*, Study Guide ed. (Leiden: Brill, 2002), 2:679–80.

14. Gregory K. Beale, "Eden, the Temple, and the Church's Mission in the New Creation," *Journal of the Evangelical Theological Society* 48 (2005): 6–8.

15. "Ezer Kenegdo," *God's Word to Women* (blog), accessed January 26, 2024, https://godswordtowomen.org/ezerkenegdo.htm; Sarah E. Fisher, "Helper: Defining the Ezer Woman," *Hebrew Word Lessons* (blog), May 13, 2018, https://hebrewwordlessons.com/2018/05/13 /helper-defining-the-ezer-woman/; Jo Saxton, "Woman, Thy Name Is Ezer," *CUT Book Excerpt, IVP Press* (blog), 2012, https:// www.ivpress.com/Media/Default/Press-Kits/3651-press.pdf; Carolyn Custis James, "Jesus and Women: The Ezer-Warriors," *FaithGateway* (blog), accessed January 26, 2024, https:// faithgateway.com/blogs/christian-books/jesus-women-ezer -warriors; John Eldredge, "God Is Our Ezer," *Wild at Heart* (blog), April 16, 2023, https://wildatheart.org/daily-reading /god-our-ezer.

16. Carmen Joy Imes, *Being God's Image: Why Creation Still Matters* (Downers Grove, IL: IVP Academic, 2023), 37. *'Ezer* is primarily used in military contexts and is best translated "ally."

17. The three examples outside of Genesis 2:18, 20 that do not refer to the Lord as helper are Isaiah 30:5; Hosea 13:9; and Daniel 11:34.

18. Victor P. Hamilton, *The Book of Genesis 1–17*, New International Commentary on the Old Testament Series, 3rd printing ed. (Grand Rapids, MI: Eerdmans, 1990), 147–48; Iain Provan, *Discovering Genesis: Content, Interpretation, Reception* (Grand Rapids, MI: Wm. B. Eerdmans Publishing Co., 2016), 78; Fabry, Heinz-Josef, "עלצ–*Ṣēlāʿ*," in *Theological Dictionary of the Old Testament* (Grand Rapids, MI: Eerdmans, 2003), 402–4; Wilda C. Gafney, *Womanist Midrash: A Reintroduction to the Women of the Torah and the Throne* (Louisville, KY: Westminster John Knox Press, 2017), 21; Anne Lapidus Lerner, *Eternally Eve: Images of Eve in the Hebrew Bible, Midrash, and Modern Jewish Poetry*, 1st ed. (Waltham, MA: Brandeis University Press, 2007), 40 and 183n102; Robert Davidson, *Genesis 1–11* (Cambridge: Cambridge University Press, 1973), 71–72.

19. Ilana Pardes, *Countertraditions in the Bible: A Feminist Approach*, NULL ed. (Cambridge, MA: Harvard University Press, 1992), 13.

20. William E. Phipps, *Genesis and Gender: Biblical Myths of Sexuality and Their Cultural Impact* (New York, NY: Praeger, 1989), 19–20.

21. Anne Lapidus Lerner, *Eternally Eve: Images of Eve in the Hebrew Bible, Midrash, and Modern Jewish Poetry*, 1st ed. (Waltham, MA: Brandeis University Press, 2007), 1.

22. Wilda C. Gafney, *Womanist Midrash: A Reintroduction to the Women of the Torah and the Throne* (Louisville, KY: Westminster John Knox Press, 2017), 21.

23. John Monson, "The Architecture of Solomon's Temple" (Manuscript, 2023), 1–2. Monson states, "The Hebrew Bible contains over one hundred words related to architecture and building. Most of these lexemes are associated with the Jerusalem temple as it is described in 1Kgs 6–7; 2 Chr 3–4, and Ezek 40–43."

24. Heinz-Josef Fabry, "עלצ–*Ṣēlāʿ*," in *Theological Dictionary of the Old Testament* (Grand Rapids: Eerdmans, 2003), 12:402–405. See also Lerner, *Eternally Eve*, 40 and 183n102.

25. Victor P. Hamilton, *The Book of Genesis 1–17*, New International Commentary on the Old Testament Series, 3rd printing ed. (Grand Rapids: Eerdmans, 1990), 178; Robert Davidson, *Genesis 1–11* (Cambridge: Cambridge University Press, 1973), 71–72.

26. See also Hamilton, *The Book of Genesis 1–17*, 147–48; Iain Provan, *Discovering Genesis: Content, Interpretation, Reception* (Grand Rapids: Eerdmans, 2016), 78; Gordon H Matties and Tremper Longman III, "7521 עלץ," in *New International Dictionary of the Old Testament Theology & Exegesis*, ed. Willem A. VanGemeren (Grand Rapids: Zondervan, 1997), 811; Davidson, "Earth's First Sanctuary," 72; see also Basil Wilberforce, *Sermons Preached in Westminster Abbey* (London: Paternoster, 1898), 103–4.

27. Davidson, "Earth's First Sanctuary," 72.

Chapter 3: Redemption Hope Through the Woman

1. Henri Blocher, *In the Beginning: The Opening Chapters of Genesis* (Downers Grove, IL: IVP, 1984), 96.

2. Jacob L. Wright, *Why the Bible Began: An Alternative History of Scripture and Its Origins* (New York: Cambridge University Press, 2023), 357.

3. Carmen Joy Imes, "Eve's Legacy Is Both Sin and Redemption," *Christianity Today*, April 19, 2023, https://www.christianitytoday .com/ct/2023/mayjune/eve-legacy-sin-redemption-mother -genesis.html.

4. Katharine C. Bushnell, *God's Word to Women: One Hundred Bible Studies on Women's Place in the Divine Economy* (North Collins, NY: Ray B. Munson, 1923), 29–30.

5. Tim Mackie, "Does God Punish Women with Pain in Childbirth?," Bible Project Classroom: Genesis, posted April 18, 2023, by BibleProject, YouTube, https://www.youtube.com/watch?v=h _zIJt0Kpes&t=8s.

6. Iain Provan, "Pain in Childbirth? Further Thoughts on 'An Attractive Fragment' (1 Chronicles 4:9–10)," in *Let Us Go Up to Zion: Essays in Honour of H. G. M. Williamson on the Occasion of His Sixty-Fifth Birthday*, ed. Iain Provan and Mark Boda (Leiden: Brill Academic, 2012), 294; see also Tim Mackie, "Does God Punish Women with Pain in Childbirth?," https://www.youtube .com/watch?v=h_zIJt0Kpes&t=8.

7. Provan, 290; John H. Walton, "Genesis," in *Zondervan Illustrated*

*Bible Backgrounds Commentary Volume 1: Genesis, Exodus,
Leviticus, Numbers, Deuteronomy* (Grand Rapids: Zondervan,
2009), 227, internal quote taken from Walton.

8. Carol Meyers, *Rediscovering Eve: Ancient Israelite Women in
Context*, 1st ed. (Oxford: Oxford University Press, 2012), 92. Meyers
demonstrates that mental anguish is a more accurate translation
than pain.

9. Iain Provan, *Discovering Genesis: Content, Interpretation, Reception*
(Grand Rapids: Eerdmans, 2016), 88.

10. The root word *'atsab*, is used also in 2 Sam 19:1–2 and Isa 54:6;
and the related root *'otseb* in Prov 15:1 and 147:2–3. See Provan,
"Pain in Childbirth?," 290–94.

11. See Gen 12:10–20; 26:1–17.

12. Kenneth A. Mathews, *Genesis 1–11:26: The New American
Commentary* (Nashville: Holman Reference, 1996), 265.

13. Gordon John Wenham, *Genesis 1–15*, ed. David Allen Hubbard,
Glenn W. Barker, and John D. W. Watts, Word Biblical
Commentary 1 (Grand Rapids: Zondervan Academic, 2014), 101–2.

14. See Ludwig Koehler et al., *The Hebrew and Aramaic Lexicon of
the Old Testament* (Leiden: E.J. Brill, 1994–2000), 1112–1113; for
example "—a. I have obtained a man with Yahweh" or "—b. I have
created (or produced) a man together with Yahweh."

15. The NET Bible notes, "There are two homonymic verbs with
this spelling, one meaning 'obtain, acquire' and the other
meaning 'create' (see Gen 14:19, 22; Deut 32:6; Ps 139:13; Prov
8:22)" (especially in Ugaritic and Phoenician). See Biblical Studies
Press, *The NET Bible First Edition Notes* (Biblical Studies Press,
2006), Gen 4:1. However, nearly every use in the Pentateuch is the
former, "to obtain, acquire, or purchase." See Mathews, *Genesis
1–11:26*, 1.265; and Nahum M. Sarna, *The Jewish Publication
Society Torah Commentary: Genesis*, 1st ed. (Philadelphia, PA:
Jewish Publication Society, 2001), 32.

16. Henry Barclay Swete, *The Old Testament in Greek: According to the
Septuagint* (Cambridge, UK: Cambridge University Press, 1909),
Gen 4:1.

17. Sarna, *The JPS Torah Commentary: Genesis*, 32. See also Wenham, *Genesis 1–15*, 101.

18. Wenham, 101–102.

19. Sarna, *The JPS Torah Commentary: Genesis*, 32.

20. Enosh is first used to refer to humanity (or mortals) in Deu 32:26, then in Job (18x); Psalms (12x, esp note Ps 90:3 Prayer of Moses); and Isaiah (8x).

21. Mathews, *Genesis 1–11:26*, 290.

22. Abraham Kuyper, *Women of the Old Testament*, trans. Henry Zylstra, 4th ed. (Zondervan, 1933), 5.

23. Kuyper, 8.

24. Biblical Studies Press, *The NET Bible First Edition Notes* (Biblical Studies Press, 2006), Gen 4:26. See Wenham, *Genesis 1–15, Volume 1*, 116.

25. Werner Herman Franzmann, *Bible History Commentary: Old Testament*, electronic ed. (Milwaukee, WI: Wisconsin Evangelical Lutheran Synod, 1980), 62–63. See Abraham (Gen 12:8; Gen 13:4; and 21:33), Isaac (Gen 26:25), Moses (Exod 33:19), David (2 Sam 6:18; 1 Chr 16:2), Elijah (1 Kgs 18:24, 32, 36).

26. The hope of *one who would come* to deliver humanity from our grief and toil is spoken by Noah's father: "He named him Noah [which sounds like the Hebrew word for *comfort* or *rest*] and said, 'He will comfort us in the labor and painful toil ['iṣābôn] of our hands caused by the ground the LORD has cursed'" (Gen 5:29). His words are clear allusions to the events in the garden (Gen 3:15–17).

CHAPTER 4: SARAH BRINGS LIFE FROM DEATH

1. Gen 22:18; 26:5; Rom 4:12–22; Gal 3:6; Jam 2:21.

2. Jacob L. Wright, *Why the Bible Began: An Alternative History of Scripture and Its Origins* (New York, NY: Cambridge University Press, 2023), 364.

3. Nahum M. Sarna, *The JPS Torah Commentary: Genesis*, 1st ed. (Philadelphia, PA: Jewish Publication Society, 2001), 94–95.

4. Marten Stol, *Women in the Ancient Near East*, trans. Helen

Richardson and M. E. J. Richardson (Boston, MA: De Gruyter, 2016), 167–69.

5. Stol, 167–69.; Eugene Merrill, "Sarah: Taking Things into Her Own Hands or Seeking to Love?," in *Vindicating the Vixens: Revisiting the Sexualized, Vilified, and Marginalized Women of the Bible*, ed. Sandra Glahn (Grand Rapids, MI: Kregel Publications, 2017), 163–65; James B. Pritchard, ed., *Ancient Near Eastern Texts Relating to the Old Testament with Supplement*, 3rd ed. (Ann Arbor, MI: Princeton University Press, 1969), 160.

6. Celina Durgin and Dru Johnson, *The Biblical World of Gender: The Daily Lives of Ancient Women and Men* (Eugene, OR: Cascade, 2022), 36.

7. Tony Maalouf, *Arabs in the Shadow of Israel: The Unfolding of God's Prophetic Plan for Ishmael's Life* (Grand Rapids: Kregel Academic, 2003), 51–53.

8. Tony Maalouf, "Hagar: God Names Adam, Hagar Names God," in *Vindicating the Vixens: Revisiting Sexualized, Vilified, and Marginalized Women of the Bible*, ed. Sandra L. Glahn (Grand Rapids: Kregel Publications, 2017), 176.

9. Maalouf, "Hagar," 175.

10. Wilda C. Gafney, *Womanist Midrash: A Reintroduction to the Women of the Torah and the Throne* (Louisville, KY: Westminster John Knox Press, 2017), 42.

11. Maalouf, "Hagar," 181.

12. See Maalouf, "Hagar," 180, quoting B. Jacob, *The First Book of the Bible, Genesis*, trans. and ed. Ernest I. Jacob and Walter Jacob (New York: KTAV Publishing, 1974), 107.

13. For more insights about Ishmael's legacy, see Maalouf, *Arabs in the Shadow of Israel*.

14. The field and cave of Machpelah facing Mamre, which are in Hebron, were purchased by Abraham (Gen 23:1–20).

CHAPTER 5: TAMAR IN THE TRANSFORMATION OF JUDAH

1. For example, Jon Bloom, "Prostitutes, Mistresses, and the Messiah: Seven Great Women of Ill Repute," *Desiring God* (blog),

December 7, 2018, https://www.desiringgod.org/articles
/prostitutes-mistresses-and-the-messiah; and Bruce K. Waltke
and Cathi J. Fredricks, *Genesis: A Commentary*, 1st ed. (Grand
Rapids: Zondervan Academic, 2001), 508.

2. For example, Exod 28:4; 29:5, 8; 39:27; 40:14; Lev 8:7, 13; 10:5; 16:4;
Ezr 2:69; Neh 7:69, 71.

3. Megan Sauter, "Judah's Pledge to Tamar: The Significance of
Judah's Signet, Cord, and Staff in Genesis 38," *Biblical Archaeology
Review*, October 27, 2021, https://www.biblicalarchaeology.org
/daily/judahs-pledge-to-tamar/.

4. Jennifer Andruska, "'Rape' in the Syntax of 2 Samuel 11:4,"
Zeitschrift für die Alttestamentliche Wissenschaft 129, no. 1 (2017):
106.

5. Ellen Van Wolde, "Does *'innâ* Denote Rape? A Semantic Analysis
of a Controversial Word," *Vetus Testamentum* (October 2002).

6. John Goldingay, *Genesis*, Baker Commentary on the Old Testament:
Pentateuch (Grand Rapids: Baker Academic, 2020), 582–83.

7. David D. Pettus, "Tamar, Daughter-in-Law of Judah," in *The Lexham
Bible Dictionary*, ed. John D. Barry et al. (Bellingham, WA: Lexham
Press, 2016).

8. Ingrid Faro, *Evil in Genesis: A Contextual Analysis of Hebrew
Lexemes for Evil in the Book of Genesis*, Studies in Scripture &
Biblical Theology (Bellingham, WA: Lexham Press, 2021), 207–9.

9. Goldingay, *Genesis*, 582–83.

10. Marten Stol, *Women in the Ancient Near East* (Boston: De Gruyter,
2016), 297.

11. Claude F. Mariottini, *Those Amazing Women of Ancient Israel*
(Grand Rapids: Kregel Academic, forthcoming), chapter 34.

12. Stol, *Women in the Ancient Near East*, 296.

13. Raymond Westbrook, "Property and the Family in Biblical Law,"
Journal for the Study of the Old Testament 113 (Sheffield, UK: JSOT
Press, 1991), 87; see also Ching Sueng Belinda Tan, "Tamar Is
Righteous, but Judah Is Not: A Narrative Analysis of Genesis 38"
(Thesis, Singapore, Singapore Bible College, 2017), 31.

14. Sarah Shectman, *Women in the Pentateuch: A Feminist and*

Source-Critical Analysis, bilingual ed. (Sheffield: Sheffield Phoenix Press Ltd, 2009), 106.

15. Zohar Amar and Naama Sukenik, "The Signs That Bind: Why Tamar Requested Judah's Signet, Cord, and Staff," *Biblical Archaeology Review* (Fall 2021), https://www.baslibrary.org /biblical-archaeology-review/47/3/22.

16. Amar and Sukenik, "Epistles: The Signs That Bind;" see Millard, *New International Dictionary of Old Testament Theology and Exegesis*, 2:324; Fouts, *New International Dictionary of Old Testament Theology and Exegesis*, 2:924–25.

17. Esther Fuchs, "The Literary Characterization of Mothers and Sexual Politics in the Hebrew Bible," *Semeia* (1989), 161.

18. Carol L. Meyers, "Was Ancient Israel a Patriarchal Society?," *Journal of Biblical Literature* 133 (2014): 16.

19. John Goldingay, *Old Testament Theology: Israel's Gospel*, reprint ed. (IVP Academic, 2015), 503.

20. Goldingay, *Old Testament Theology: Israel's Gospel*, 266.

21. Tan, "Tamar Is Righteous," 17.

22. Tan, "Tamar Is Righteous," 17–18; quoting Gerhard von Rad, *Old Testament Theology, Volume I: A Commentary*, trans. D. M. G. Stalker (Louisville, KY: Westminster John Knox Press, 2001), 373.

23. Von Rad, *Old Testament Theology, Volume I*, 1:374.

24. Tan, "Tamar Is Righteous," 17–18.

25. Tan, "Tamar Is Righteous," from the abstract (no page number).

CHAPTER 6: WOMEN WHO INSTIGATE THE EXODUS

1. Jacqueline E. Lapsley, *Whispering the Word: Hearing Women's Stories in the Old Testament*, annotated ed. (Louisville, KY: Westminster John Knox Press, 2005), 72. The word "harshness" appears twice in verses 13–14, and "the root for 'labor' appears five times, pounding into the reader the severity of the oppression."

2. Lapsley, *Whispering the Word*, 69; I lift the use of "transgressive" from Lapsely's perceptive exegesis.

3. Carol Meyers, *Rediscovering Eve: Ancient Israelite Women in Context*, 1st ed. (Oxford: Oxford University Press, 2012), 98–99.

4. Meyers, 99.

5. Lapsley, *Whispering the Word*, 71.

6. Lapsley, 73.

7. Lapsley, 74.

8. Victor Harold Matthews, Mark W. Chavalas, and John H. Walton, *The IVP Bible Background Commentary: Old Testament*, electronic ed. (Downers Grove, IL: InterVarsity Press, 2000), Exod 2:3.

9. Robert Jamieson, A. R. Fausset, and David Brown, *Commentary Critical and Explanatory on the Whole Bible*, vol. 1 (Oak Harbor, WA: Logos Research Systems, Inc, 1997), 48, gives ten to twelve years old based on the use of the Hebrew noun *'almâ*. However, Jewish traditional sources provide she was six to seven years old; Tamar Meir, "Miriam: Midrash and Aggadah," *The Shalvi/ Hyman Encyclopedia of Jewish Women* (blog), May 17, 2024, 48, https://jwa.org/encyclopedia/article/miriam-midrash-and-aggadah.

10. Lapsley, *Whispering the Word*, 74.

11. Carmen Joy Imes, "Freedom Fighters of Exodus," in *The Biblical World of Gender: The Daily Lives of Ancient Women and Men*, ed. Celina Durgin and Dru Johnson (Eugene, OR: Cascade Books, 2022), 39–45.

12. Brian D. Russell, *The Song of the Sea: The Date of Composition and Influence of Exodus 15:1–21* (New York: Peter Lang, 2007), 59–73.

13. Lapsley, *Whispering the Word*, 87.

CHAPTER 7: RAHAB'S FAITH PREPARES THE WAY INTO THE PROMISED LAND

1. Hélène Dallaire, *Joshua*, ed. Tremper Longman III and David E. Garland, rev. ed., The Expositor's Bible Commentary (Grand Rapids: Zondervan Academic, 2017), Josh 1.

2. Richard S. Hess, *Joshua: An Introduction and Commentary*, ed. D. J. Wiseman, illustrated ed., Tyndale Old Testament Commentaries (Downers Grove, IL: IVP Academic, 2008), Josh 2:1–24.

3. Michael A. Fishbane, *Haftarot: The JPS Bible Commentary* (Philadelphia, PA: Jewish Publication Society, 2002), 229; see

also Gene M. Tucker, "The Rahab Saga (Joshua 2): Some Form-Critical and Traditio-Historical Observations," in *The Use of the Old Testament in the New*, ed. J. M. Erfird (Chapel Hill, NC: Duke University Press, 1972), 66–86.

4. David M. Howard, *Joshua: An Exegetical and Theological Exposition of Holy Scripture*, vol. 5, The New American Commentary (Nashville: Holman Reference, 1998), 93.

5. Ching Sueng Belinda Tan, "Tamar Is Righteous, but Judah Is Not: A Narrative Analysis of Genesis 38" (Thesis, Singapore, Singapore Bible College, 2017), 46; and Yairah Amit, *Reading Biblical Narratives: Literary Criticism and the Hebrew Bible*, trans. Yael Lotan (Minneapolis, MN: Augsburg Fortress, 2001), 119. Shittim is in the land of Moab, in the Transjordan across from Jericho (Num 33:48–49).

6. Howard, *Joshua*, 5:93.

7. For example, Biblical Studies Press, *The NET Bible First Edition Notes* (Biblical Studies Press, 2006), Jos 2:3; see also Mariottini, *Those Amazing Women of Ancient Israel*, draft p. 150; and Irene Nowell, *Women in the Old Testament*, 3rd printing ed. (Collegeville, MN: Liturgical Press, 1997), 60.

8. Howard, *Joshua*, 5:93–94. In agreement, see also Dallaire, *Joshua*, 91–92.

9. Marten Stol, *Women in the Ancient Near East* (Boston: De Gruyter, 2016), 399–404.

10. Leila Leah Bronner, *From Eve to Esther: Rabbinic Reconstructs of Biblical Women*, 1st ed. (Louisville, KY: Westminster John Knox Press, 1994), 148.

11. Stol, *Women in the Ancient Near East*, 408.

12. Bronner, *From Eve to Esther*, 149.

13. Fishbane, *Haftarot: The JPS Bible Commentary*, 231.

14. Athalya Brenner, *The Israelite Woman: Social Role and Literary Type in Biblical Narrative*, repr, The Biblical Seminar 2 (Sheffield: JSOT Press, 1994), 80; see also Dallaire, *Joshua*, 93.

15. Howard, *Joshua*, 5:93.

16. Dallaire, *Joshua*, 91.

17. Nowell, *Women in the Old Testament*, 60.

18. Thomas B. Dozeman, *Joshua 1–12: A New Translation with Introduction and Commentary*, ed. John J. Collins, vol. 6b, The Anchor Yale Bible (New Haven: Yale University Press, 2015), 223–25.

19. L. Daniel Hawk, *Every Promise Fulfilled: Contesting Plots in Joshua* (Eugene, OR: Wipf and Stock, 2009), 59–71.

20. Robert Polzin, *Moses and the Deuteronomist: A Literary Study of the Deuteronomic History: Part 1 : Deuteronomy/Joshua/Judges*, 1st THUS ed., Indiana Studies in Biblical Literature (Bloomington, IN: Indiana Univ Press, 1993), 86.

21. Hess, *Joshua*, Joshua 2:1–24.

22. Andrzej Toczyski, *The 'Geometrics' of the Rahab Story: A Multi-Dimensional Analysis of Joshua 2*, The Library of Hebrew Bible/Old Testament Studies 664 (New York: T&T Clark, 2018), 169.

23. Hess, *Joshua*, Joshua 2:1–24.

24. D. G. Firth, "Joshua 24 and the Welcome of Foreigners," *Acta Theologica* 38, no. 2 (2018), 74.

25. Firth, 78.

26. Hess, *Joshua*, Josh 5:13–6:27.

27. Firth, "Joshua 24 and the Welcome of Foreigners," 75.

28. Firth, 76.

29. Firth, 80.

30. Carmen Joy Imes, "Reading the Bible with Women," *Christianity Today*, March 13, 2024, https://www.christianitytoday.com /2024/03/rahab-prostitute-jericho-joshua-study-bible-women -history/.

31. Walter Bauer et al., *A Greek-English Lexicon of the New Testament and Other Early Christian Literature: Based on Walter Bauers's "Griechisch-Deutsches Wörterbuch Zu Den Schriften Des Neuen Testaments Und Der Frühchristlichen Literatur," 6th Ed*, 3rd ed (Chicago: the University of Chicago Press, 2000), 99, "disobedience is always toward God, God's ordinances, or revelation."

32. Imes, "Reading the Bible with Women," 5.

Chapter 8: Deborah Leads, and Jael Drives the Victory Home

1. Tamar Kadari, "Deborah 2: Midrash and Aggadah," in *The Shalvi/ Hyman Encyclopedia of Jewish Women*, ed. Paula Hyman and Dalia Ofer, Jewish Women's Archive (Moshe Shalvi, 2017), https://jwa.org /encyclopedia/article/deborah-2-midrash-and-aggadah.

2. Mercedes L. García Bachmann et al., *Judges*, ed. Barbara E. Reid OP and Ahida Pilarski (Collegeville, MN: Liturgical Press, 2018), 45.

3. Ron Pierce, "Deborah: Only When a Good Man Is Hard to Find?," in *Vindicating the Vixens: Revisiting Sexualized, Vilified, and Marginalized Women of the Bible*, ed. Sandra L. Glahn (Grand Rapids: Kregel Publications, 2017), 191.

4. Wayne A. Grudem, *Evangelical Feminism & Biblical Truth: An Analysis of More Than One Hundred Disputed Questions*, reprint ed. (Wheaton, IL: Crossway, 2012), 134.

5. Leila Leah Bronner, *From Eve to Esther: Rabbinic Reconstructs of Biblical Women*, 1st ed. (Louisville, KY: Westminster John Knox Press, 1994), 171; see also Pierce, "Deborah," 191.

6. Thomas R. Schreiner, "The Valuable Ministries of Women in the Context of Male Leadership: A Survey of Old and New Testament Examples and Teaching," in *Recovering Biblical Manhood and Womanhood: A Response to Evangelical Feminism*, ed. John Piper and Wayne A. Grudem, revised (Wheaton, IL: Crossway, 2021), 292.

7. Mark J. Boda, "Recycling Heaven's Words: Receiving and Retrieving Divine Revelation in the Historiography of Judges," in *Prophets and Prophecy and Ancient Israelite Historiography*, ed. Mark J. Boda and Lissa Wray Beal (Winona Lake, IN: Eisenbrauns, 2013), 50–51.

8. Susan Niditch, *Judges: A Commentary*, The Old Testament Library (Louisville, KY: Westminster John Knox Press, 2008), 60.

9. Richard S. Hess, "Israelite Identity and Personal Names from the Book of Judges," *Hebrew Studies* 44 (2003): 26.

10. Robin Baker, *Hollow Men, Strange Women: Riddles, Codes and Otherness in the Book of Judges* (Leiden: Brill Academic Pub, 2016), 96.

11. Gordon D. Fee and Douglas K. Stuart, *How to Read the Bible for All Its Worth*, 4th ed. (Grand Rapids: Zondervan, 2014), 188.

12. Victor H. Matthews, *Judges and Ruth*, annotated ed., New Cambridge Bible Commentary (Cambridge, UK: Cambridge University Press, 2004), 65.

13. Boda, "Recycling Heaven's Words," 51.

14. Michelle Knight, "The Prophet's Song of Victory: Judges 5 Within a Trajectory of Theological Training in the Book of Judges," *Bulletin for Biblical Research* 33, no. 4 (2023): 449–50, https://doi.org/10.5325/bullbiblrese.33.4.0441.

15. Matthews, *Judges and Ruth*, 65.

16. Niditch, *Judges*, 65.

17. Abraham Kuyper, *Women of the Old Testament*, trans. Henry Zylstra, 4th ed. (Zondervan, 1933), 74.

18. Robert Jamieson, A. R. Fausset, and David Brown, *Commentary Critical and Explanatory on the Whole Bible*, vol. 1 (Oak Harbor, WA: Logos Research Systems, Inc, 1997), 1:160; Niditch, *Judges*, 60.

19. Pierce, "Deborah: Only When," 194.

20. Baker, *Hollow Men, Strange Women*, 51; see also Bachmann et al., *Judges*, 44.

21. Carolyn Pressler, *Joshua, Judges and Ruth* (Louisville, KY: Westminster John Knox Press, 2002), 155.

22. Matthews, *Judges and Ruth*, 64.

23. Knight, "The Prophet's Song of Victory," 449–50. See also Bachmann et al., *Judges*, 44; and *HALOT*, 1623.

24. Jamieson, Fausset, and Brown, *Commentary Critical and Explanatory on the Whole Bible*, 1:160.

25. Jamieson, Fausset, and Brown, 1:160.

26. Susan Ackerman, *Warrior, Dancer, Seductress, Queen: Women in Judges and Biblical Israel*, 1st ed. (New York: Anchor Bible, 1998), 37.

27. Claudia V. Camp, "The Wise Women of 2 Samuel: A Role Model for Women in Early Israel?," *Catholic Biblical Quarterly* 43 (1981): 27–28. See also Ackerman, *Warrior, Dancer, Seductress, Queen*, 40–42.

28. Ackerman, *Warrior, Dancer, Seductress, Queen*, 39.

29. Ackerman, 39, (italics original); see footnote 34: "compare *villages,* literally, 'daughters,' in Num 21:25, 32; Josh 15:45; Judg 11:26"; Ackerman is quoting from W. F. Stinespring and B. O. Long, "Annotations on 2 Samuel," in *The New Oxford Annotated Bible,* ed. B. M. Metzger and R. E. Murphy (New York: Oxford University Press, 1991), 414.

30. J. Cheryl Exum, "'Mother in Israel': A Familiar Figure Reconsidered," in *Feminist Interpretation of the Bible,* ed. Letty M. Russell (Philadelphia, PA: Westminster Press, 1985), 85.

31. Michael Snearly, "Kenites," in *The Lexham Bible Dictionary,* ed. John D. Barry et al. (Lexham Press, 2016).

32. Mariottini, *Those Amazing Women of Ancient Israel,* forthcoming, draft 157.

33. Baker, *Hollow Men, Strange Women,* 51–53.

34. Knight, "The Prophet's Song of Victory," 454.

35. Michelle Knight, "Geometry and Psalmody: Characterization and the Role of Deborah's Song (Judges 5)," in *"Now These Records Are Ancient": Studies in Ancient Near Eastern and Biblical History, Language and Culture in Honor of K. Lawson Younger,* ed. James K. Hoffmeier et al., vol. 114, Ägypten Und Altes Testament (Münster: Zaphon, 2022), 295.

36. Niditch, *Judges,* 76.

37. Knight, "The Prophet's Song of Victory," 452, 454.

38. Knight, 451.

39. Ackerman, *Warrior, Dancer, Seductress, Queen,* 31.

40. Knight, "The Prophet's Song of Victory," 455.

41. Knight, "The Prophet's Song of Victory," 455.

42. Knight, "The Prophet's Song of Victory," 456.

43. Knight, 442.

44. Knight, 442–44.

45. Tammi J. Schneider, *Berit Olam: Judges,* ed. David W. Cotter and Berit Olam (Collegeville, MN: Liturgical Press, 2000), 9.

46. Matthew J. Lynch, "The Roots of Violence: Male Violence against Women in Genesis," in *The Biblical World of Gender: The Daily Lives of Ancient Women and Men,* ed. Celina Durgin and Dru

Johnson (Eugene, OR: Cascade Books, 2022), 92–93, (italics original).

47. Bronner, *From Eve to Esther*, 174.

Chapter 9: Ruth, a Woman of Valor and Loyal Love

1. Daniel Isaac Block, *Ruth: A Discourse Analysis of the Hebrew Bible*, ed. Daniel Isaac Block, Zondervan Exegetical Commentary on the Old Testament (Grand Rapids: Zondervan, 2015), 83.

2. Block, *Ruth*, 60.

3. R. P. Nettelhorst, "Love," in *Lexham Theological Wordbook*, ed. Douglas Magnum et al., Lexham Bible Reference Series (Bellingham, WA: Lexham Press, 2014), (bold original).

4. Block, *Ruth*, 95; see also Ruth 4:15.

5. Edward Fay Campbell Jr, *Ruth: A New Translation with Introduction, Notes, and Commentary*, Nachdr., The Anchor Bible 7 (New Haven, CT: Yale University Press, 2011), 74; as Campbell states, "*Thus may Yahweh do to me, / And thus may he add, / If even death will separate / Me from you.* This solemn oath formulary appears only here and in eleven passages in Samuel and Kings. The first part of it was presumably accompanied by a symbolic gesture, something like our index finger across the throat."

6. Marnie Legaspi, "Ruth: The So-Called Scandal," in *Vindicating the Vixens: Revisiting Sexualized, Vilified, and Marginalized Women of the Bible*, ed. Sandra Glahn (Grand Rapids.: Kregel Academic, 2017), 78.

7. Koehler, Baumgartner, and Stamm, *HALOT*, 1994–2000, 311.

8. Gene M. Tucker, "The Rahab Saga (Joshua 2): Some Form-Critical and Traditio-Historical Observations," in *The Use of the Old Testament in the New*, ed. J. M. Erfird (Chapel Hill, NC: Duke University Press, 1972), 31.

9. Gale A. Yee, "Ruth," in *Fortress Commentary on the Bible*, 354.

10. "The term *levirate* refers to the legal case in Deuteronomy 25:5–10"; Benjamin Kilchör, "Levirate Obligation in the Hebrew Bible," in *Biblical Studies* (Oxford University Press, 2022), https://doi.org/10.1093/obo/9780195393361-0296.

11. Koehler, Baumgartner, and Stamm, *HALOT*, 1994–2000, 169 (emphasis original).

12. Benjamin Kilchör, "Levirate Obligation in the Hebrew Bible," in *Oxford Bibliographies* (Oxford University Press, March 23, 2022).

13. Yee, "Ruth," 354.

14. Block, *Ruth*, 165.

15. For example, George M. Schwab, "Ruth," in *The Expositor's Bible Commentary: Numbers-Ruth*, ed. Tremper Longman III and David E. Garland, rev. ed., vol. 2 (Grand Rapids: Zondervan, 2012), 1324, 1332, 1335.

16. Block, *Ruth*, 171–72, 178–85.

17. Koehler, Baumgartner, and Stamm, *HALOT*, 1994–2000, 486.

18. Adele Berlin, "Ruth—Big Theme, Little Book," *Biblical History Daily* (blog), July 30, 2024, https://www.biblicalarchaeology.org/daily/biblical-topics/hebrew-bible/the-story-of-ruth/.

19. Yee, "Ruth," 356.

20. Jean Louis Ska, "'Our Fathers Have Told Us': Introduction to the Analysis of Hebrew Narratives," *Subsidia Biblica* 13 (Roma: Editrice Pontificio Instituto Biblico, 1990), 29.

21. Block, *Ruth*, 183.

22. Robert L. Hubbard Jr., "The *Go'el* in Ancient Israel: Theological Reflections on an Israelite Institution," *Bulletin for Biblical Research* 1 (1991): 11–12.

23. Block, *Ruth*, 205.

24. Block, 233.

25. Carolyn Custis James, *The Gospel of Ruth: Loving God Enough to Break the Rules* (Grand Rapids: Zondervan, 2011), 66.

CHAPTER 10: HANNAH'S PRAYER CHANGES HISTORY

1. Joan E. Cook, "Hannah's Desire, God's Design: Early Interpretations of the Story of Hannah," *Journal for the Study of the Old Testament* 282 (Sheffield, UK: Sheffield Academic, 1999), 21.

2. Graeme Auld, *1 and 2 Samuel*, ed. James D. G. Dunn and John W. Rogerson, Eerdmans Commentary on the Bible (Grand Rapids: Eerdmans, 2003), 214.

3. Michelle Knight, "The Prophet's Song of Victory: Judges 5 Within a Trajectory of Theological Training in the Book of Judges," *Bulletin for Biblical Research* 33, no. 4 (2023): 442.

4. T. Desmond Alexander, "Royal Expectations in Genesis to Kings: Their Importance for Biblical Theology," *Tyndale Bulletin* 49, no. 2 (1998): 194–98.

5. Alexander, 198.

6. Cook, *Hannah's Desire, God's Design*, 13.

7. Cheryl You, "The Historian's Heroines: Examining the Characterization of Female Role Models in the Early Israelite Monarchy," *Journal of Biblical Perspectives in Leadership* 9, no. 1 (Fall 2019), 179.

8. *NIV Bible Speaks Today: Notes* (London: InterVarsity Press, 2020), 350.

9. Johanna W. H. van Wijk-Bos, *The Road to Kingship: 1–2 Samuel*, vol. 2: A People and a Land (Grand Rapids: Eerdmans, 2020), 26.

10. Biblical Studies Press, *The NET Bible First Edition Notes* (Biblical Studies Press, 2006), 1 Sam 1:10.

11. John D. Barry et al., *Faithlife Study Bible* (Bellingham, WA: Lexham Press, n.d.), 1 Sam 1:11. See Num 21:2 and Judg 11:30–31; for Nazarite vow see Num 6:5.

12. Barry, 1 Sam 1:11; her husband did not later try to deter or nullify her vow (see Num 30:6–15).

13. Leora Jackson, "Hannah as a Precedent-Setter," *Jewish Women's Archive* (blog), September 16, 2010, https://jwa.org/blog/hannah.

14. Robert Jamieson, A. R. Fausset, and David Brown, *Commentary Critical and Explanatory on the Whole Bible*, vol. 1 (Oak Harbor, WA: Logos Research Systems, Inc, 1997), 1:176.

15. Auld, *1 and 2 Samuel*, 214.

16. Michael A. Fishbane, *Haftarot: The JPS Bible Commentary* (Philadelphia, PA: Jewish Publication Society, 2002), 374.

17. Auld, *1 and 2 Samuel*, 214.

18. *The NET Bible First Edition Notes*, 1 Sam 1:20.

19. Auld, *1 and 2 Samuel*, 214.

20. Victor Harold Matthews, Mark W. Chavalas, and John H. Walton, *The IVP Bible Background Commentary: Old Testament*, electronic

ed. (Downers Grove, IL: InterVarsity Press, 2000), 1 Sam 1:22–24;
see also Bryan E. Beyer, "1 Samuel," in *CSB Study Bible: Notes*,
ed. Edwin A. Blum and Trevin Wax (Nashville: Holman Bible
Publishers, 2017), 413; and Stephen J. Andrews and Robert D.
Bergen, *1, 2 Samuel*, vol. 6 in Holman Old Testament Commentary
(Nashville: Holman Reference, 2009), 16.

21. Albert Barnes, *Notes on the Old Testament: 1 Samuel to Esther*, ed.
F. C. Cook and J. M. Fuller (London: John Murray, 1879), 8.

22. Ralph W. Klein, *1 Samuel*, ed. Glenn W. Barker, David Allen
Hubbard, and D. W. Watts, 2nd ed., vol. 10, Word Biblical
Commentary (Waco, TX: Word Books, 2017), 19.

23. Auld, *1 and 2 Samuel*, 215.

24. You, "The Historian's Heroines," 180; Walter Brueggemann,
"2 Samuel 21–24: An Appendix of Deconstruction?," *Catholic
Biblical Quarterly* 50, no. 3 (July 1988): 397.

25. Leila Leah Bronner, *Stories of Biblical Mothers: Maternal Power
in the Hebrew Bible* (Lanham, MD: University Press of America,
2004), 31.

26. Jacob L. Wright, *Why the Bible Began: An Alternative History of
Scripture and Its Origins* (New York: Cambridge University Press,
2023), 286.

27. Fishbane, *Haftarot: The JPS Bible Commentary*, 376–77.

28. Fishbane, 376–77.

29. You, "The Historian's Heroines," 179.

30. Mary J. Evans, *The Message of Samuel: Personalities, Potential,
Politics and Power*, ed. Alec Motyer and Derek Tidball, The Bible
Speaks Today (Downers Grove, IL: InterVarsity Press, 2004), 24–25.

31. You, "The Historian's Heroines," 179.

32. Koowon Kim, *1 Samuel*, ed. Federico G. Villanueva et al., Asia Bible
Commentary (Carlisle, UK: Langham Global Library, 2018), 6.

Chapter 11: Recovering Bathsheba's Dignity

1. Sara M. Koenig, *Isn't This Bathsheba? A Study in Characterization*,
vol. 177, Princeton Theological Monograph (Eugene, OR: Wipf and
Stock, 2011), 5.

2. Cheryl You, "The Historian's Heroines: Examining the Characterization of Female Role Models in the Early Israelite Monarchy," *Journal of Biblical Perspectives in Leadership* 9, no. 1 (Fall 2019), 190.

3. Tamar Kadari, "Bathsheba: Midrash and Aggadah," *Jewish Women's Archive* (blog), accessed August 31, 2024, https://jwa.org/encyclopedia/article/bathsheba-midrash-and-aggadah.

4. Elna K. Solvang, "A Woman's Place Is in the House: Royal Women of Judah and Their Involvement in the House of David," *Journal for the Study of the Old Testament Supplement Series* 349 (London: Sheffield Academic, 2003), 133.

5. You, "The Historian's Heroines," 190.

6. Brent Nessler, "Tracing Bathsheba's Metamorphosis through the Lens of Trauma and Recovery," *Journal of Biblical Literature* 142, no. 1 (2023): 95.

7. Randall C. Bailey, *David in Love and War: The Pursuit of Pursuit of Power in 2 Samuel 10–12* (London: Bloomsbury Publishing, 2009), 88.

8. George G. Nicol, "The Alleged Rape of Bathsheba: Some Observations on Ambiguity in Biblical Narrative," *Journal for the Study of the Old Testament* 22, no. 73 (March 1, 1997): 44, https://doi.org/10.1177/030908929702207303.

9. Bailey, *David in Love and War*, 88.

10. Robert Alter, *The Art of Biblical Narrative*, 2nd ed. (New York: Basic Books, 2011), 95.

11. Moshe Garsiel, "The Story of David and Bathsheba: A Different Approach," *Catholic Biblical Quarterly* 55 (1993): 255.

12. Amihai Mazar, *Archaeology of the Land of the Bible 10,000–586 B.C.E*, Anchor Bible Reference Library, vol. 1 (New York: Doubleday, 1992), 486; Oded Borowski, *Daily Life in Biblical Times*, Archaeology and Biblical Studies 5 (Atlanta: Society of Biblical Literature, 2003), 16–20; see also Avraham Faust, "Purity and Impurity in Iron Age Israel," *Biblical Archaeology Review* 45, no. 2 (2019): 36–43, 60, 62.

13. J. Cheryl Exum, *Plotted, Shot and Painted: Cultural Representations*

of Biblical Women, Gender, Culture, Theory 3 (Sheffield, UK: Sheffield Academic, 1996), 19–53.

14. Ludwig Koehler et al., *The Hebrew and Aramaic Lexicon of the Old Testament* (Leiden: E.J. Brill, 1994–2000), 1220.

15. Caryn Tamber-Rosenau, "Biblical Bathing Beauties and the Manipulation of the Male Gaze: What Judith Can Tell Us about Bathsheba and Susanna," *Journal of Feminist Studies in Religion* 33, no. 2 (2017): 55.

16. Mignon R. Jacobs, "Mothering a Leader: Bathsheba's Relational and Functional Identities," in *Mother Goose, Mother Jones, Mommie Dearest: Biblical Mothers and Their Children*, ed. Gale A. Yee, Cheryl A Kirk-Duggan, and Tina Pippin, *Semeia Studies* 61 (Atlanta, GA: Society of Biblical Literature, 2009), 70.

17. Nessler, "Tracing Bathsheba's Metamorphosis," 97.

18. Morris Jastrow Jr. et al., "Bath-Sheba," in *The Jewish Encyclopedia Online*, 1906, https://www.jewishencyclopedia.com/articles/2659 -bath-sheba.

19. Garsiel, "The Story of David and Bathsheba: A Different Approach," 253.

20. Nessler, "Tracing Bathsheba's Metamorphosis," 97.

21. Sandie Gravett, "Reading 'Rape' in the Hebrew Bible: A Consideration of Language," *Journal for the Study of the Old Testament* 28, no. 3 (2004): 280.

22. Nessler, "Tracing Bathsheba's Metamorphosis," 97.

23. Graeme Auld, *1 and 2 Samuel*, ed. James D. G. Dunn and John W. Rogerson, Eerdmans Commentary on the Bible (Grand Rapids: Eerdmans, 2003), 453.

24. Ingrid Faro, *Evil in Genesis: A Contextual Analysis of Hebrew Lexemes for Evil in the Book of Genesis*, Studies in Scripture & Biblical Theology (Bellingham, WA: Lexham Press, 2021), 97–132.

25. Jennifer Andruska, "'Rape' in the Syntax of 2 Samuel 11:4," *ZAW* 129, no. 1 (2017): 106.

26. Andruska, 106. In 2 Samuel, "to take" occurs seven times, and all indicate taking by force of an unwillingly other (8:1, 7, 8; 9:5; 10:4; 11:4; 12:30). For example, when the Ammonite leader

"takes" David's envoys, humiliates them, and sends them away; and when David "takes" the crown off the head of the king of the Ammonites after capturing their city and puts it on his own head (2 Sam 10:4; 12:30). See also, Auld, *1 and 2 Samuel*, 455.

27. You, "The Historian's Heroines," 190.

28. Solvang, "A Woman's Place Is in the House," 133.

29. Nessler, "Tracing Bathsheba's Metamorphosis," 97.

30. J D'ror Chankin-Gould et al., "The Sanctified 'Adulteress' and Her Circumstantial Clause: Bathsheba's Bath and Self-Consecration in 2 Samuel 11," *Journal for the Study of the Old Testament* 32, no. 3 (2008): 349, https://doi.org/10.1177/0309089208090805.

31. J D'ror Chankin-Gould et al., "The Sanctified 'Adulteress,'" 342, 347.

32. Chankin-Gould et al., 345.

33. Chankin-Gould et al., 349, and citing K Kautzsch, ed., *Gesenius' Hebrew Grammar* (New York: Oxford University Press, 1910), 453.

34. Koehler, Baumgartner, and Stamm, *HALOT*, 1994–2000, 1073, in the *qal* stem.

35. Chankin-Gould et al., "The Sanctified 'Adultress,'" 347–48.

36. Chankin-Gould et al., 350.

37. Nessler, "Tracing Bathsheba's Metamorphosis," 94.

38. You, "The Historian's Heroines," 191.

39. Solvang, "A Woman's Place Is in the House," 134.

40. Karen Strand Winslow, *1 & 2 Kings: A Commentary in the Wesleyan Tradition*, New Beacon Bible Commentary (Kansas City, MO: Beacon Hill Press of Kansas City, 2017), 45.

41. You, "The Historian's Heroines," 192.

42. Koehler, Baumgartner, and Stamm, *HALOT*, 1994–2000, 755.

43. Winslow, *1 & 2 Kings*, 2b of 121.

44. Winslow, 2b of 121.

45. Mignon R. Jacobs, "Mothering a Leader: Bathsheba's Relational and Functional Identities," in *Mother Goose, Mother Jones, Mommie Dearest: Biblical Mothers and Their Children*, ed. Gale A. Yee, Cheryl A Kirk-Duggan, and Tina Pippin, *Semeia Studies* 61 (Atlanta, GA: Society of Biblical Literature, 2009), 79.

46. Winslow, *1 & 2 Kings*, 2c of 121.

47. Andrew C. Bowling, "1 Kings," in *CSB Study Bible: Notes*, ed. Edwin A. Blum and Trevin Wax (Nashville: Holman Bible Publishers, 2017), 506.

48. Matthews, Chavalas, and Walton, *The IVP Bible Background Commentary: Old Testament*, 1 Kgs 2:13–21.

49. Gary Inrig, *1 & 2 Kings*, ed. Max Anders, Holman Old Testament Commentary / General Ed.: Max Anders 7 (Nashville: Broadman & Holman, 2003), 16 (bold in original).

50. Nessler, "Tracing Bathsheba's Metamorphosis," 108. ("implicity" added to the quote)

51. Nessler, 93.

52. You, "The Historian's Heroines," 193.

53. Jacobs, "Mothering a Leader: Bathsheba's Relational and Functional Identities," 81.

54. Chankin-Gould et al., "The Sanctified 'Adultress.'"

55. Annalaura Montgomery Chuang, "Formed by War," *Christianity Today*, May 28, 2015, http://www.christianitytoday.com/ct/2015/june/formed-by-war-ptsd.html.

56. Robert Alter, *Ancient Israel: The Former Prophets: Joshua, Judges, Samuel and Kings; A Translation with Commentary*, 1st ed. (New York: Norton, 2013), 600.

57. Jacobs, "Mothering a Leader: Bathsheba's Relational and Functional Identities," 71.

CHAPTER 12: JEHOSHEBA SAVES THE LINE OF DAVID

1. Ginny Brewer-Boydston, "Athaliah, Queen of Judah," in *Lexham Bible Dictionary*, ed. John D. Barry et al. (Bellingham, WA: Lexham Press, 2016); see also Athalya Brenner, *The Israelite Woman: Social Role and Literary Type in Biblical Narrative*, repr, The Biblical Seminar 2 (Sheffield: JSOT Press, 1994), 207.

2. Werner Herman Franzmann, *Bible History Commentary: Old Testament*, electronic ed. (Milwaukee, WI: Wisconsin Evangelical Lutheran Synod, 1980), 486.

3. Wilda C. Gafney, *Womanist Midrash: A Reintroduction to the Women of the Torah and the Throne* (Louisville, KY: Westminster John Knox Press, 2017), 257.

4. Gary Inrig, *1 & 2 Kings*, ed. Max Anders, Holman Old Testament Commentary / General Ed.: Max Anders 7 (Nashville: Broadman & Holman, 2003), 276.

5. John D. Barry et al., *Faithlife Study Bible* (Bellingham, WA: Lexham Press, n.d.), 2 Ki 11:2; See 2 Chr 22:11 and 2 Chr 24:6–7.

6. Karen Strand Winslow, *1 & 2 Kings: A Commentary in the Wesleyan Tradition*, New Beacon Bible Commentary (Kansas City, MO: Beacon Hill Press of Kansas City, 2017), 47 of 121.

7. Winslow, 47 of 121.

8. Winslow, 45 of 121.

Epilogue

1. Trent C. Butler, *Holman New Testament Commentary: NIV Based. Vol. 3: Luke / Author: Trent C. Butler*, ed. Max Anders, Nachdr., vol. 3 (Nashville, TN: Holman Reference, 2007), 12.

2. Douglas Mangum, ed., *Lexham Context Commentary: New Testament* (Bellingham, WA: Lexham Press, 2020), Luke 1:46–56.

3. Alfred Plummer, *The Gospel According to St. Luke* (London: Bloomsbury T&T Clark, 1989), 72, https://doi.org/10.5040/9781472556776.

4. JoAnn Ford Watson, "Phanuel (Person)," in *The Anchor Yale Bible Dictionary*, ed. David Noel Freedman (New York: Doubleday, 1992), 288.

5. Ben Witherington III, "Anna (Person)," in *The Anchor Yale Bible Dictionary*, 257.

6. John D. Barry et al., *Faithlife Study Bible* (Bellingham, WA: Lexham Press, n.d.), Mt 27:56. "This could be Jesus' mother, His aunt, or another Mary not mentioned elsewhere in the Gospels (compare Mark 6:3; 15:40; John 19:25)."

7. Walter W. Wessel, *The Expositor's Bible Commentary: Matthew, Mark, Luke*, ed. Frank E. Gaebelein, vol. 8 (Grand Rapids:

Zondervan Publishing House, 1984), 8784. Salome is "Zebedee's wife and the mother of James and John (cf. Matt 27:56)."

8. Jon Courson, *Jon Courson's Application Commentary* (Nashville: Thomas Nelson, 2020), 595–96; see also "Witness," *Jewish Virtual Library: Ancient Jewish History* (blog), accessed February 25, 2025, which states, "By the method of gezerah shavah, it is derived from Scripture that only men can be competent witnesses," https://www.jewishvirtuallibrary.org/witness.

9. Nijay K. Gupta, *Tell Her Story: How Women Led, Taught, and Ministered in the Early Church* (Downers Grove, IL: IVP Academic, 2023); and see Lynn H. Cohick and Amy Brown Hughes, *Christian Women in the Patristic World: Their Influence, Authority, and Legacy in the Second Through Fifth Centuries* (Grand Rapids: Baker Academic, 2017).

Suggested Readings

Durgin, Celina, and Dru Johnson, eds. *The Biblical World of Gender: The Daily Lives of Ancient Women and Men*. Eugene, OR: Cascade Books, 2022.

Glahn, Sandra, ed. *Vindicating the Vixens: Revisiting Sexualized, Vilified, and Marginalized Women of the Bible*. Grand Rapids, MI: Kregel Academic, 2017.

Gupta, Nijay K. *Tell Her Story: How Women Led, Taught, and Ministered in the Early Church*. Downers Grove, IL: IVP Academic, 2023.

Lapsley, Jacqueline E. *Whispering the Word: Hearing Women's Stories in the Old Testament*. Annotated edition. Louisville, KY: Westminster John Knox Press, 2005.

Meyers, Carol. *Rediscovering Eve: Ancient Israelite Women in Context*. 1st edition. Oxford: Oxford University Press, 2012.

You, Cheryl. "The Historian's Heroines: Examining the Characterization of Female Role Models in the Early Israelite Monarchy." *Journal of Biblical Perspectives in Leadership*, Fall 2019.

General Index

Scripture Index